UFOs and ALIENS
'New Zealand Through the Years'

Ufos and Aliens in New Zealand

MOIRA McGHEE

UFOs and Aliens – New Zealand Through the Years

Reports of UFOs and Aliens in New Zealand.

INUFOR books may be purchased for business, educational or sales promotional use. For information address: INUFOR. P.O. Box 169, Katoomba N.S.W. 2280 Australia.

INUFOR Web Sites; www.independentnetuforesearchers.com.au. www.facebook.com/inufor.
Email: ind.net.ufo.res@bigpond.com

First INUFOR Paperback Edition published in January 2024

ISBN-978-0-9587-045-2-6

CONTENTS

INTRODUCTION

This book is dedicated to Fred, Phyllis and Bryan Dickeson, without whom this book, based on much of their work, would not have been possible. The Dickeson family were slightly old fashioned, in the fact that they supported the traditional values of honesty and trustworthiness. They were committed Christians, with Fred being a warden at his local church. In 1954, Fred and Phyllis were early pioneers in New Zealand ufology, and their interest and research continued for many decades.

In a letter to a journalist colleague, Fred Dickeson wrote; *'Like most people interested in UFOs nowadays, a general interest in aerial phenomena developed at an early age.*

'During the 1930's, my first secondary school days were spent at Wellington College. I was living with my grandmother and uncle, who was the Commanding Officer of the N.Z. Permanent Air Force. When the Air Board was formed soon after the NZPAF became the RNZAF, Uncle then became the Controller of Civil Aviation in N.Z. (Group Captain T.M. Wilkes M.C.)

'At this time, the novelty of aircraft was still sufficient to strain public credibility in such a military venture, - it was the era of flying history, being in the middle of exciting pioneer times of Kingsford Smith, Ulm, Jean Batten, the Tasman crossings etc.

'It was probably inevitable, when World War II began I joined the Photographic Section of the RNZAF at Whenuapai in 1940. I spent two years in Fiji, returned to Whenuapai and transferred to Woodbourne Photographic Section, where I met my wife for the first time. After being demobbed from Wigram in 1945, we went back to Kaikohe, Northland, my old home town, where we carried on professional photography. We moved to Timaru – my wife's home town, in 1950.

'Then, in 1954, we read Desmond Leslie and George Adamski's book 'Flying Saucers have Landed'. The idea of extraterrestrial intelligence intrigued us both. We wrote to Adamski. Information was exchanged on a regular basis between Timaru and Mt. Palomar, and to help him out we agreed to form the 'Adamski Correspondence Group'.

At the end of the 1960s, having become disillusioned with George Adamski, they changed the name of their group to the *'Scientific Approach to Cosmic Understanding'* and continued on with serious research, liaison and investigation activities. In 1978, they summed up their early impressions of the situation;

'In the early 1950s, pioneers in the field were mostly quite gullible, believing that the UFO visitors were friendly, coming from outer space to help mankind. It was idealistic, all 'brotherly love, peace and harmony'. The thought of rebuilding a grand new world for humanity, with their guidance and knowledge, was a beautiful concept, especially after the chaos of World War II.

'It was also the period of satellites and space probes, first venturing into space, going to the Moon and ushering in the Space Age – all very exciting and an era of great hope and promise. During this time, the rivalry between the two super-powers, America and Russia, increased in the space-race, each making claims as they advanced....the race was on. So too, was the 'Cold War' between the big powers, when atomic tests were carried out, all too frequently on a gigantic scale.'

Even though some people were having contact with friendly humanoid beings, there were already some disturbing incidents in our skies, and then came the more evil 'Greys' and accounts of people being injured, or abducted from their homes and subjected to unpleasant medical procedures.

By the end of the 1960s, the benevolent aspect was fast fading, and entering a more sinister stage, as hostile reports accelerated. The 'Good Old Days' of trust and innocence were coming to an end.

The Dickesons also had some more wise words to say; *'Another point to be considered also was, that man's historic Epic of the Moon landing in July 1969, closed the decade, and brought new dimensions to the Space Age and the Sixties to a dramatic conclusion, paving the way for further probes into space.*

'It also proved that our Solar System planets were not inhabited by beings like ourselves. This was a great blow to many who once thought or were told we were being visited by Venusians, Martians etc. There are, however, quite a number still clinging to this concept, who cannot accept scientific findings that these planets are not inhabited by beings like ourselves.'

Like the Dickesons, I moved on to a new era of research, however I could not dismiss the thought that these visitors may have bases on other planets within our Solar System.

Their son, Bryan, was educated at Christchurch University, attaining both a Bachelor of Science and a Bachelor of Arts. Upon graduation, he moved to Wellington where he was employed from 1976 to 1977 with the Ministry of Agriculture and in 1978 as an Assistant Advisory Officer at the Head Office of the Department of Scientific and Industrial Research. During these years he was a great help to his parents in the research and investigation into UFO reports. From an early age he assisted with the production of their newsletters and magazines, which were distributed to their own group members, and other researchers around the world.

Bryan moved to Sydney in 1979, and I met him at a conference in the mid-eighties. We soon became working colleagues, and he joined with me in the formation of 'The Independent Network of UFO Researchers'. Later, in 1991, along with Paul Sowiak, we founded 'UFO Research N.S.W.', an organisation which is still thriving due to Bryan's hard work and dedication in the early days.

In 1996, Bryan and I investigated a 'UFO Flap' on the N.S.W. Central Coast, and co-authored our book 'The Gosford Files'.

In addition to his contribution to New Zealand ufology, over the last forty years Bryan has devoted a great deal of time and effort to investigating and researching countless incidents in Australia. For years he produced, edited and published the magazine 'UFO Reporter', and wrote most of the articles. He organised the early meetings and conferences, plus field trips. Often he travelled long distances to interview witnesses, and examine sighting areas.

Unlike today, when many groups just post sighting reports on the internet, we would venture out to interview witnesses, taking our notebooks, cameras, tape recorders, Geiger counters and specimen jars with us. The Dickesons, and many of their colleagues, would also conduct very thorough investigations.

When asked about his approach to the subject, Bryan said; "When I use scientific methods in my work, I get very interesting results, so I've always been surprised that more scientists haven't got involved in ufology hands-on. There are tremendous opportunities to do some good physics in ufology, and these are being ignored. Both science and ufology suffer because of this lack of involvement, which is largely an historical accident.

"....Fortunately, in recent years, the laws of physics have taken on some very interesting ideas. For example, over the past fifty years UFO investigators have accumulated many witness reports about the natural phenomenon of ball lightning. Scientists have only recently come to recognize ball lightning as a bona fide phenomenon, and their explanation is surprisingly similar to what we were discussing twenty or thirty years ago. I also remember my parents, forty years ago, discussing life elsewhere in the Universe as a common occurrence, and SETI scientists are now doing this also. These changes and developments enhance both science and ufology."

New Zealand and its early history of 'visitors' from the sky.

New Zealand is only a small country, comprising of two main large islands, and situated far away from other populations in the southern oceans of our globe. Even so, it still had its share of unidentified aerial phenomena.

In the earlier twentieth century, prior to the end of World War 2, the New Zealand population was very conservative, and very few reports were made of unidentified aerial craft.

One was received, by author Michael Hervey, in later years. Bertrand Collins told of how, one day in 1934, whilst on his farm in Ashley Clinton, he and his wife saw a white disc passing overhead. It was about twenty to twenty-five feet in diameter, at an altitude of 1,000ft, and had an intense bright golden centre, around which the whitish part rotated. It moved to the east, then came around in a curve before suddenly shooting up and disappearing.

One of the first indications the early colonists had, of the possibility of the indigenous population interacting with 'visitors from the skies', came in 1869. '*NSSRNZ*' documented this interesting occurrence.

'Colonial army officer, Colonel St. John, was engaged in a campaign against Te Kooti and his followers. At the close of the day's skirmishes in the Urewera Hills, the Colonel and his company of the Te Arawa Loyalists decided to make a camp for the night at Nga Hukeke Pa at Te Tahora in the Ruatahuna Valley. The peace of the camp was to be disturbed by a strange occurrence, which Colonel St. John duly recorded;

'Just about dusk, I heard a great hullabaloo and rushed out of the whare, (Maori hut), thinking that there might be some fresh Hauhau, (tribal enemies), move, and found our native allies grovelling on the ground and singing out lustily.

'Near the top of the wooded range, on the right, a large ball of fire was slowly wending its way down the vale. It was quite round, seemed to be about six feet in diameter, emitted a dull light and was unaccompanied by the slightest noise; presently, it turned round a corner and was lost to sight.'

The colonel regarded it as a false alarm, but apparently the Maoris believed it was a prophecy of disaster from their God – the great Atua. As it turned out, St. John won the battle the next day.

The Colonel recorded another incident when a similar object was sighted coming from the sea, sailing up the valley and entering the Waioeka Gorge, where it was lost from sight; *'Similar terror struck the natives. There were a number of friendly natives present on this occasion also, and I saw one of them, a brave man as I well knew, throw himself on the ground...groaning and moaning in dread.'*

In fact, long before European settlement, well over two centuries ago, the Maoris had a long history, recited or passed on in chants, of possible alien visitation.

One legend speaks of a 'flying man', Tama-rua, and the loud report, like the sound of a gun, that at was heard whenever he departed, in an appearance similar to a meteor.

New Zealand researcher, Vic Harris, who wrote at length about the Maori mythology, noted that one description of how to identify a god, suggested an object with a plexiglass-like dome, and four legs suspended from it. He went on to say ; *'The great Polynesian voyager, Toi, was said to have deserted his first wife, Te Kura, when she bore a son to a god, Tama-i-waho, who descended to earth and came from Hawaiki by means of flying through the air.*

'A description of another god, Hau-ki-waho, could almost be that of a man dressed in a space suit. He was said to have no nose, no forehead and no eyebrows. He did not resemble a human being, but was 'all flat', not having any prominent parts,' just like the face of a cliff'. Nothing could be seen save the eyeholes, the opening of the mouth, and those of the ears and the nostrils.

He was said to have ascended into the heavens, and returned to earth, bringing much knowledge and information about things unknown to the Maori.

'...With regards to astronomical recording by the Maoris, 'Rongomai' was the name given to a body that moved through space and appeared to give off sparks. 'Unahiroa' was a similar phenomenon, with an exceedingly small body, with rays or appendages like smoke. The Maoris were aware that the earth was round and not flat, and the Maori Tohongas, (a type of wise-man), were said to be able to list more than three hundred stars by name, and knew the secrets of levitation. According to their traditions, our Solar System has twelve planets, Jupiter had bands, Saturn rings, and the Pleiades seven stars.

'A myth of the Ngati Awa tribe from around Whakatane, told how a maiden went to a stream to get water, when there shone all around her a great blaze of light. She saw no human form, but on the sunny water fell the shadow of a man, who told her that when she had a male child, she was to call it Awa-nui-a-rangi, the river of light.

'Another myth, 'Uenuku' and 'Hine-pukohu-rangi', the 'Mist Maiden', has similar connotations. The 'Mist Maiden' only goes to live with the 'Uenuku' during the night, and disappears at dawn. She forbids 'Uenuku' to tell his people until a child is born to them, but he disregards this, and she leaves him forever. A column of mist is seen slowly descending from the heavens. It envelops her, and she disappears.

CHAPTER ONE

THOSE ELUSIVE AIRSHIPS

The majority of airship sightings in New Zealand occurred between July and September 1909, however this was not the first time these elusive craft had been reported in other parts of the world.

Count Ferdinand von Zeppelin began work on his prototype in 1898, however it was several years before he achieved even a modest success. In 1907 one effort was applauded for reaching the speed of 36mph.

It wasn't just in Europe that experimental 'craft' were being devised. In 1897, when the 'airships' were first being seen in the United States, there were only a few, crude prototypes in existence, certainly nothing that could match the aerodynamic design, speed and manoeuvrability of the craft being reported.

In 1896, an attorney announced to the newspapers, that he was about to lodge a patent for a new airship of revolutionary design, which operated on compressed air. However, it seems nobody actually got to view this invention.

In April 1897, two Indiana farmers, Jeremiah Collier and William York, claimed that they had happened upon an airship, sitting on Wood Patch Hill, which had apparently been damaged. The crew, who were effecting repairs, said it belonged to E.J. Pennington, who later confirmed this, saying that he owned three such machines.

About the same time, in Illinois, two farmhands, John Halley and Adolf Wenke, saw a similar object come in to land at about 9pm. They went and spoke to the pilot, who was quite friendly, and said he was the inventor of the craft, which he only flew at night, along with his 'crew' – his wife and another man. After explaining that he was anxious to keep the propulsion system a secret, he climbed back aboard, and the airship took off, and was soon lost from sight.

By 1909, there were some modest successes with monoplanes, biplanes and airships. Louis Bleriot had flown from Calais to Dover, and Graf von Zeppelin had launched his sixth airship and founded the world's first commercial airline company. The U.S. government had bought its first aeroplane from the Wright Brothers for $30,000

Bryan Dickeson, realising that most of the information pertaining to New Zealand had been lost in the mists of time, searched old libraries and newspaper offices from one end of the country to the other, uncovering much of the missing data from 1909.

He discovered that the majority of sightings were from a distance, however some witnesses had a much closer view.

On 24th July, a Saturday night, several boys were playing on the beach at Kaka Point, when they saw a huge, illuminated object, as big as a house, moving about in the air. Residents noted that it had also been sighted on a few previous nights. It illuminated the roof of a nearby house, and the lads fled in fright. The strange craft glided close to the rocks at the old pilot station, before disappearing shortly after.

Two days later, on July 26th, at Kelso, Dunedin, several school children along with Mrs. Russell, one of the teachers, and other witnesses saw a strange, black craft, which was described as being shaped like a boat, with what looked like a man seated in it. It approached from the direction of the Blue Mountains, circled high over the school, then returned back to the hills.

It was reported as having 'supports' or 'sails', which didn't move, on each side, a 'box' underneath, and a fast rotating wheel at the back. It was travelling fairly fast at first, but slowed when it turned and came lower. Six of the young witnesses independently drew strikingly similar sketches of what they had seen.

Two days earlier, a dozen tradesmen who were working just out of Kelso, watched a cigar-shaped airship which had a large headlight, and carriage suspended below.

Pukepeto 27th July 1909

The *'Clutha Leader'* detailed how Allen Mitchell and Alex Riach, while working at Lambourne, saw a large boat-shape structure, with what seemed like a long pole on top, high in the air over 'Messrs Begg Bros'. at Pukepeto. They thought it was coming straight for them, and would pass overhead, but it dipped and swayed up and down, with an 'easy motion', before swerving to the left, and crossing the river before it was lost from sight.

The next night, a resident of North Eastern Valley, Dunedin, was woken by a peculiar noise, he first thought to be an earthquake. He got up and saw a 'big black thing', with a searchlight attached, floating up over Knox College.

Two days later, on the early morning of 30th July, an airship came down near a dredge working on the river in the Waikaka Valley, north of Gore. *The 'Gore Standard'* reported that at about 5am, two lights broke through the mist, and the witnesses saw the forms of two figures sitting in the strange object which suddenly appeared. The craft, which was narrow and 'boat-shaped', moved quite fast, at times slowing as it dipped and rose. They watched for some time, until it shot up into the mist, leaving a yellow glare. It was seen again in a gap in the direction of Otakamara before finally disappearing.

The night before, passengers from the Hokitika train had crowded onto the platform at the Nelson Creek Station to watch a lighted 'airship' come inshore, and descend over the breakers before moving off, against a strong wind, to Point Elizabeth.

'The Mataura Ensign' of Gore reported that only a couple of days later, in the early hours of the morning, at Greendale, a farmhand was feeding the horses when there was a strange whirring sound which seemed to frighten the animals. He looked up to see a 150ft long airship overhead. It was moving extremely fast, and had head and tail lights. Two other local residents reported strange aerial craft that day.

On 3rd August, the Napier *'Hawkes Bay Herald'* published an account from their Waipawa correspondent; *'A circumstantial story is being eagerly discussed in Waipawa of the seeing of an airship by a Waipawa man on Tuesday night. He was riding near the racecourse and his horse became restless. He discovered as the cause that a large torpedo-shaped structure was passing over his head.*

'The airship, he states, was painted grey, and three persons were visible, one of whom shouted out to him in an unknown tongue. The ship rose to a great height, showing lights at prow and stern, and after circling around, disappeared behind a hill.

'On the same night, another resident saw a ship-like structure high in the air, whence proceeded a humming sound. The ship was so high that it appeared only a yard or so long. A faint light came from the ship. Another resident

9

asked her husband, about the same hour that night; "..what is that humming noise?" Others are also coming forward with evidence of seeing lights etc. Generally, however, the stories are all being received with the greatest scepticism.'

On August 5th, a correspondent of the *'Wanganui Chronicle'* wrote that he had seen an airship whilst passing over the Wanganui bridge at about 11.30pm; *'I distinctly saw a large airship flying down the river from Aramoho, and passed out of sight in the direction of Castlecliff. It was flying at a height of 200ft, and I could distinctly see its two large wings, which made a hissing sound. I calculate it was travelling at ninety miles an hour, at least. It had a powerful light in the front, and also one on either side.'*

Investigator, Henk Hinfelaar, noted that never, at any stage, was more than one object sighted at the same time. He said that the shape of the object was usually described as being an elongated –'torpedo', 'boat', 'cigar' or 'codfish'.

'In some cases, always at night, the objects carried strong searchlights, (with reflectors), which lit up the landscape for miles. The speed of the craft was varied, and ranged from a cruising speed of 30mph to great velocity. Their passage through our skies was frequently described as the sailing of a boat, or as the rising and falling of a bird in flight. Some of the craft put on quite a display while dipping from 2,000ft to 1,000ft and circling around.

'...Although in one particular case, the papers took great delight in reporting an obvious hoax, in all other cases ridicule and rigorous cross-examination failed to shake the accounts as reported by hundreds of witnesses.'

Although the authorities and sometimes the newspapers tried to 'play the matter down', in 1909 there was some consternation due to the possibility of war with Germany, which of course did occur only a few years later. A couple of witnesses, at Port Molyneux, had also reported an airship with occupants who spoke something similar to Japanese.

Some residents were already forecasting an extraterrestrial invasion. One 'W.H.T.' wrote to the *'Dunedin Star';* *'I have been surprised at the simplicity of the general public in regard to this popular topic of conversation. The inventor of a new flying machine would not be likely to experiment with it in the dark rather than in the daytime, nor would the owner of such a machine find any pleasure in aerial locomotion on cold winter nights. An aerial invasion of New*

Zealand by Germans or Japs is not probable, and in any case, the invaders would have attacked Wellington or Dunedin before appearing at Cromwell or Kaitangata.

'To me, it seems more likely to be the beginning of an invasion from Mars. Water being scarce on that planet, the Martians are necessarily looking out for a new world to inhabit, and New Zealand, being a conspicuous object on our globe, they will probably attack us first....'

The 'Oamuru Mail' of July 30th, had a more sensible approach, but did make some valid comments; 'There is something uncanny about the rumours that airships are hovering over the earth in the extreme north and south of this country. Airships appear, just at the moment, to be in the air. The trouble is that, not unusually, they have not cared to keep there, but have been victims of the law of gravitation, (this is a reference to the Zeppelin experiments in Germany).

'But the samples which have adorned the heavens in New Zealand appear to be less given to this fault of instability than those which have been produced in the world's great centres. Ours, according to all accounts, are amenable to absolute control. They show no tendency to fall and break themselves into kindling wood. The wonder is, why, if with comparatively slender resources of knowledge, mechanical ability and money, New Zealand inventors of flying machines can succeed so well as made out, difficulty is still experienced in the Old World in making them safe and effective.'

Bryan Dickeson noted that after September 1909, there were few, if any, airship sightings. He wrote; ' The New Zealand wave was preceded, as is now known, by similar sightings in Britain, during March, April and May, and the U.S.A. experienced similar sightings from December 1909 well into 1910. In 1913 unidentified dirigible-shaped objects visited Southern England, and in 1914 South Africa. Prior to 1909, sightings of unidentified airship-type objects were made over New Mexico in 1880, and all over the U.S.A, in 1896 and 1897.

'It is significant that the early sighting waves we know of, all occurred over English-speaking countries. It seems possible that the great wave which occurred between 1909 and 1914, was in fact world-wide in nature, the lack of information from other countries being due possibly to the fact that records of such early sightings probably do not exist in many of the less developed societies of Asia, Africa and the Middle East.'

There is no doubt that these unidentified craft, and strange lights, were being sighted by a multitude of people, but it is more likely, on the balance of probabilities, that they were one or more earthly prototypes. However, they may have been extraterrestrial, we just don't know, there is no proof either way.

CHAPTER TWO

N.Z. RESEARCH GROUPS AND INVESTGATORS

Over the years, there have been many UFO researchers in New Zealand, and several organisations with their own investigators. Many had a history of service in the Air Force, and by 1960, were conducting their own investigations into UFO sighting reports both locally and all over the country.

'The Civilian Saucer Investigation (NZ)' – 'CSI'

The *'CSI'* was founded by RNZAF Sergeant Harold Fulton in October 1952. Originally, it was a closed group, associated with the personnel of the Air Force Base at Whenuapai, however it was opened up to public subscription the following year. Fulton had been corresponding with his U.S. counterparts since the end of World War 2, when many airmen had sighted the infamous 'Foo-Fighters'.

He soon organised a nationwide network of investigators and reporters, and produced their own newsletter – *'Flying Saucers'* – later to be renamed – *'Spaceview'*. In 1953, U.S. contactee, George Adamski, published his first book, *'Flying Saucers Have Landed'*, which attracted the formation of 'Flying Saucer Clubs' in the U.S. and a great deal of interest in New Zealand. At first, Fulton supported Adamski, but after his New Zealand lecture tour in early 1959, Fulton's enthusiasm waned, and as he began to question many of Adamski's claims, the co-existence between *'CSI'* and the Adamski organisations ceased. In September 1959, when Fulton was posted to Singapore for two years, *'CSI'* went into hibernation.

In 1957, Henk Hinfelaar, who had been a member of *'CSI'* since 1955, formed a new group in Henderson, independent of *'CSI'*, mainly to also distribute and promote information coming from contactee George Adamski in the USA. They continued their dogmatic support of Adamski long after other groups had denounced him, and this created a schism in the overall UFO research community in New Zealand.

Fred, Phyllis and Bryan Dickeson

In late 1954, Fred and Phyllis Dickeson, on the South Island, pioneered the *'Adamski Flying Saucer Group'*, later renamed the *'Adamski Correspondence*

Group'. At their instigation, Adamski made 'Question and Answer' tapes which were copied and distributed to groups, where meetings had been initiated in both the North and South Islands.

On the South Island, their 'parent' organisation met in Timaru, and by 1959 they had sponsored very active groups in Nelson, (under Reg Gledhill), Christchurch, (under Harold Hale), Invercargill, (under Russell Beck) and also Dunedin. They also established close contacts with colleagues in Australia, the United States, South Africa, Britain and Europe.

By January/ February 1959, following his visit to new Zealand, both Harold Fulton and the Dickesons had become disillusioned with George Adamski. Fred and Phyllis changed the name of their group, eventually being known as the *'Scientific Approach to Cosmic Understanding'*, (*S.A.T.C.U.*), which thrived and operated for many years after. This created a rift within the movement, as Hinfelaar, and his North Island followers, still strongly supported George Adamski.

Hinfelaar's *'S.S.R.G.'* group on the North Island conducted their own investigations, which were published in their newsletter *'Spaceview'*. In 1964 the two groups began exchanging information again, and in 1975, researcher/investigator Vic Harris took over the editorship of *'Spaceview'*.

The Tauranga UFO Investigation Group

Originally formed as an *'Adamski Correspondence Group'*, it was natured by Harvey Cooke, and a committee was formed by the members, who also organised the New Zealand UFO Conventions in 1972 and 1975.

In their publication, *'Kosmon News'* , he was invited to write a few words about himself. He noted his quest to know more about God, and try to get a better understanding of 'The Infinite Ever-Presence'. He went on to say; "Now, it was this background that helped get me involved in the UFO field.

"At the beginning of 1939, I joined the Air Force as an airframe technician, and saw eight years of service. When World War II broke out, I was among the first troops overseas as we sailed on September 6th from Wellington to Picton, to take up residence at the uncompleted Woodbourne Air Force Base. Later, I was to take more serious journeys into the Pacific area, doing two tours of duty, plus several flights into what was called the war zone."

After the war, and a short stay in Britain, he returned to New Zealand, and purchased a bookshop in Wellington. After reading books by George Adamski and Donald Keyhoe, and moving to Tauranga in 1954, he learned of the 'George Adamski Correspondence Group', and Henk Hinfelaar asked him to form a local group, which he did in 1957.

Harvey expanded the once small group into an, independent, active and vibrant organisation, which conducted investigations, held seminars, gave lectures and hosted guest speakers from near and afar. Harvey passed away, aged 88, in 2005, just three days before a celebratory event was to be given, honouring his service to ufology.

Besides his contribution to ufology in New Zealand, Harvey also supported the 'Classic Flyers' Club in Tauranga, and followed all the latest developments in aeronautical and space technologies.

Suzanne Hanson, one of New Zealand's most prominent researchers, wrote the following in a tribute to Harvey; *'One of the major, and most significant contributions Harvey has made to N.Z. ufology is in the area of active investigation. Harvey was closely involved in investigating major periods of UFO activity, including the 'Ngatea landing site', the 'Kaikoura lights' and the 'Gisborne flap, all of which attracted worldwide attention.*

..... 'Harvey was a friend and colleague of mine for over twenty years. He told me that he believed most people who study UFO phenomena eventually undergo a change in spiritual awareness, as they are forced to examine the future and this planet, and our very origins, existence and place in the Universe – alongside other beings. His speeches have always encouraged and challenged people to consider UFO related topics with common sense and scrutiny, and not to get bogged down in programmed linear thinking, to listen and discuss, but not necessarily to accept all information immediately or blindly.'

The Auckland University UFO Research Group

This group, which was initiated by Tony Brunt in 1969, produced several newsletters until 1971, but disintegrated when its leaders moved on from university. During its existence, many incidents, including the Ngatea site, were meticulously investigated.

Other Early Groups

Many other groups that were only short-lived included – *'Civilian Aerial Phenomenon Research'*, founded in 1971. which only lasted a year – and the *'Aerial Phenomenon Research Group'*, in Christchurch, which only existed in 1973-4.

A more spiritual approach was taken by Ron Birch's *'Cosmic Centre, Whangerei'*. In 1971, Brinsley Le Poer Trench, in Britain, organised, with Phil Austin, in Auckland, an offshoot of his *'Contact'* organisation, which intermittently produced a newsletter, but offered little local coverage.

Later groups and researchers included *'The New Zealand UFO Studies Group'*, *'The Unexplained Phenomena Research Society' (Te Kuiti Branch)* – under Dr. Bob Valkenburg, and later a Christchurch Branch under Prudence Buttery. Peter Hassell founded an *'Unusual Data Investigation Service'*, and later wrote the book – *'The New Zealand Files – UFOs in New Zealand'*

The Early Days

Fred Dickeson wrote these words in 1972; *'Soon after the first atomic bombs were dropped on Japanese soil in 1945, thus bringing World War II to a climax, reports of mysterious flying objects began to filter through the news media around the world.*

'These space craft proved a challenge of the unknown. Many were reported in different shapes, sizes, colours and moving at fantastic speeds in unbelievable manoeuvres. As their numbers increased, reports flooded in from people in all walks of life. This resulted in small UFO research groups springing up, in the 1950's, in various countries around the globe. These were pioneers, in a field endeavouring to unravel the truth of these visitors from space, and to solve the riddle of their existence.

'It has not been an easy road for those taking the initiative in this study – the years have been time consuming, frustrating but extremely fascinating, and in a way, rewarding. The pit-falls have been many, and the answers to endless questions as to whom, why, what and the wherefore of their appearance, still unfortunately, remain rather obscure.

'Sometimes, it appears to many in this work to be like treading warily and carefully down an unknown, unending one-way street, never knowing what one will find next. Certainly there are those who claim 'they know' – but do they? They never seem able to prove their reasoning or points of view to everyone's satisfaction. All sorts of theories and patterns have emerged, yet no true researcher can afford to be dogmatic about his or her conclusions. Have you noticed that as soon as one thinks the answer is found, something else turns up to change it?

'It is indeed regrettable that the whole UFO field seems to have become the target for sensational journalists who write for the large circulating 'glossy magazines', not forgetting TV and radio programs.

'To create 'good reading', they attempt to embellish their writings with inflated sheer nonsense, the truth being twisted and perverted to thrill the masses for excitement in unreality. Consequently, the results are – further distortion and confusion of the whole flying saucer fraternity – confusing the entire overall picture for interested 'new-comers' on the scene.

'On the other hand, enormous amounts of information are being uncovered, and evidence of UFO's actual existence continues to mount in a startling and convincing nature. Therefore, it is more important than ever for researchers, (now in their thousands), to keep a level headed, scientific approach to the subject.

'If we are to progress further in this realm, and ultimately help pave the way for recognition of these intergalactic 'beings', by all humanity on this planet – Please keep the subject SANE, strive to maintain an OPEN MIND, be FLEXIBLE and KEEP GOING, despite the many obstacles!'

Other Researchers

Bruce Cathie

Captain Bruce Cathie was born in 1930, in Auckland, and educated at Otahuhu Technical College. He became an engineering apprentice, and later joined the Royal New Zealand Air Force, and trained as a pilot. After spending three years in agricultural aviation, he joined the New Zealand National Airways corporation in 1955, where he remained, piloting many different airliners, including Boeing 737's, until his retirement in 1981.

In 1965, using the pseudonym, 'Kirkpatrick', he had reported an underwater object at Kaipara Harbour, however, in 1956, when co-pilot on a DC-3 flight from Auckland to Paraparaumu, he and the crew saw an object at an extremely high altitude in the east. Conditions were calm, with clear visibility, and they watched as it travelled in a curved trajectory from east to west, across their track, before disappearing, in a flash of light, in the area of D'Urville Island. It had travelled across New Zealand in the vicinity, or slightly to the north of Cook Strait. He later calculated it as having a diameter of 1,500ft to 2,000ft.

Having developed an interest in UFOs, over the years he contacted and liaised with various investigators and their research groups. After discovering the research conducted by Frenchman, Aime Michelle, he developed a theory that the earth had energy lines, similar to the ley lines known by our ancestors, which were being used by the 'visitors' and possibly our own military and scientists.

As the Earth spins on its axis and through space, the amount of energy generated must be enormous. Were the UFOs tapping into this energy, and was this enabled by all the edifices, standing stones and pyramids, some thousands of years old, scattered over the Earth? In Europe alone, thousands of stone monoliths mark the ley lines. In China, the Feng Shui experts recognised the powerful currents and lines of magnetism, or 'Dragon Paths', that run invisibly through the landscape and over the whole surface of the earth. Many academics and historians have hypothesised that there is a connection between some stone structures, the pyramids and extraterrestrials.

In a letter to Fred Dickeson, Cathie wrote; *'We have positive proof that the scientists have transmitting stations established all over New Zealand, and that these stations are built into the UFO grid. Woodbourne is part of the System. This has been admitted to me by an American scientist. It appears that experiments in anti-gravity are being carried out on a large scale. The scientists have direct communication with UFOs. I was warned that the scientists will stop publication of my second book, as all this information and positive proof we have, will be in it. Time will tell.'*

Bruce, whilst developing his theories on 'energy grids', devised some quite complicated, mathematical equations, which he discussed in his books – *'Harmonic 33'. 'Harmonic 695', 'The Pulse of the Universe', 'The Energy Grid'*, and *'The Bridge to Infinity'*. However, his theories, which also incorporated the occurrences of earthquakes, volcanoes and the detonation of atomic bombs, did not go unchallenged, with some experts expressing grave doubts.

Murray Stott

Murray Stott's parents had been involved in UFO research, and were on good terms with Harold Fulton. Murray considered that the Hinfellars had virtually hijacked *'CSI'* when they started their own international network correspondence role, which may have been a factor in Harold Fulton considering that his own position in the group had effectively been undermined, and his decision in 1959 to retire and go to Singapore.

A massive split, and many acrimonious words, between groups and researchers occurred when many, including Murray's parents and the Dickesons, disavowed George Adamski, and the situation even worsened when news of Mr. X and the messages he received came to the fore.

The Hinfelaars remained staunch supporters of Adamski until his death, when they ceased to be prominent in the UFO research field. Murray Stott went his separate way, conducting research and investigations of his own, eventually publishing his book, *'Aliens over the Antipodes'* in1984.

Suzanne Hanson

Suzy Hanson, now one of New Zealand's leading investigators for *'UFOCUS NZ'* has experienced contacts of her own. In her book, *'The Dual Soul Connection'*, she tells of her New Zealand childhood in the 1950s and 1960s.

Her mother's side of the family were gifted with psychic abilities, and her grandmother spoke of 'seeing balls of light, in her room, which spoke to her'. Several of her great aunts were involved in early spiritual and healing groups.

When she recalled seeing 'night visitors', - 'three small figures like glowing silhouettes', - in her room at night, her mother would tell her they were guardian angels. She felt they had taken her somewhere, but could never remember where.

As a young child, she and her family witnessed 'a glowing, orange, cigar-shaped light'.... "It was enthralling to watch this brilliant bar of orange light...It was the most exciting night of my life so far." Her parents thought that it was not caused by natural phenomena or aircraft, and said it must have come from outer space.

Suzy recalled; *"Looking back, I believe my psyche was altered in an instant by this possibility, and I viewed the night sky through a new light of discovery and potential, with a fascination that has never diminished."*

When she was twenty, Suzy and a friend, whilst driving through the countryside, north of Gisborne, noticed some bright lights in the sky. The car engine inexplicably failed, and they heard a painful, intense, 'rasping, buzzing, electronic sound'. They arrived at their destination one-and-a-half hours later than expected, and it wasn't until many years later, under hypnosis, that she recalled what had happened that night, and indeed many other times when she had been interacting with the 'Grey' aliens.

Her previously mentioned book, detailing many of the events, is well worth reading.

Dr Jan Pajak

In 1982, Dr Jan Pajak, a Polish engineering and computer specialist, moved to New Zealand, to take up a post-doctoral fellowship at Christchurch University. He later resigned, as his peers were not happy about his interest in UFOs. Not to be deterred, he announced that he had plans for a 'Magnocraft', which would resemble the oft reported 'flying saucers', and be powered by super strong electromagnets. He claimed his invention would fly at over 7,000 mph, and would enable mankind to make interstellar trips.

He later moved to Invercargill, where he tutored computer programmers, and took up a lecturing post at Dunedin University. Although he made a small hand-held model of his proposed invention, it is doubtful if his project ever reached fruition. In the meantime, he conducted his own research into the UFO phenomenon,

In the March 1991 edition of the *'Australian UFO Bulletin'*, Paul Norman from *'VUFORS'* published a very detailed article, analysing the 'Magnocraft'. Its author, Polish Dr Jan Pajak, who was, by then, attached to the New Zealand University of Otago, was convinced that all the UFO sightings over the previous twenty or more years, were due to the innovation of this amazing craft. Another saucer-shaped object, called 'Silver Bug', was being developed in the USA in

1955, and was the forerunner of more exotic prototypes. The official report on 'Project Silver Bug' was not declassified until 1995.

Other researchers around the world, were also intrigued with the developments into anti-gravity. During the 1950s, there had been rumours that we were on the brink of overcoming gravity. Canadian engineer, Wilbert Smith, had done extensive research on gravity, including the effect of nuclear weapons upon Earth's gravity field. He was also closely involved with 'Project Magnet', and spoke of 'the boys topside', and information from other undisclosed 'channels'.

When all talk of anti-gravity ceased, many experts thought that the research had become classified and gone 'black budget'. Certainly it has been developed to a considerable extent, and by the turn of the 21st century, the Mitre Corporation was hosting an 'International High-Frequency Gravitational Waves Working Group Programme'.

MUFON

The U.S. organisation – *'Mutual UFO Network'* – quickly set up branches in New Zealand, and at one time Murray Bott was the co-ordinator, and from 1996 to 2013, Glennys McKay was co-ordinating both the Australian and New Zealand groups.

Glennys McKay

Glennys, a much valued colleague of mine, founded the *'Queensland UFO Network'* in the early 1980s. Here she assisted people suffering trauma from memories of alien contact, and provided a forum for people to share their interests and experiences,

Glennys was later the Queensland Director of *'MUFON'* followed by ten years as their Australasian Director. In the late 1990s, she co-ordinated and hosted two Australian International UFO Symposiums in Brisbane, and organised another in New Zealand, providing the opportunity for international scientists and researchers to liaise and exchange information.

Glennys also participated in our 1997 *'INUFOR-MUFON- UFOR NSW Joint UFO Seminar'*, and included the following thoughts during her presentation:

'WE ARE NOT ALONE'

'Over the past two years I have worked, against all odds, to bring people together to share updated information, from many countries, about the UFO phenomena. There are powers who do not wish this information to be given out to the people. This negative power, that seems to be sweeping our planet at the present time, has made me realise more and more, the importance of raising the level of consciousness of this planet to awaken within, the knowledge that 'WE ARE NOT ALONE'.

'For the last few centuries human beings have tended to regard themselves as the only highly evolved form of intelligent life in the universe. Many developments in recent years have challenged and undermined this view.

'Too frequently, across the world, people from all walks of life are turning to the skies and reporting strange objects. Many have detailed close encounters with an alien form that seems very foreign to our belief of what people should look like.

'Over the past ten years I have been directed to go to various places, where, along with my husband and other people, we have had encounters with craft and beings who have shown themselves to us. Although much has been written about 'grey aliens', our encounters have been with people who look like us, only taller and very intelligent. We have communicated, both verbally and telepathically. One wonders if there is an almighty cover-up in regards to these people who are walking among us. Where do they come from?

'In all the years of my having communicated with them, they have expressed the importance of the people of this Earth getting back to finding our own spirituality and learning to love one another. We must save this planet from greed and destruction, and from the powers that seem hell bent on destroying what our Creator gave us. We must always remember we are the caretakers of this Earth.

'Regardless of what we are told – 'we are not alone'. If only we could all live in peace and harmony, regardless of race, colour or creed, this spiritual journey that we have begun is a never ending journey. Let us continue to find that inner peace, then we can create a domino effect throughout the Universe.'

Glennys is quite reticent about her own experiences, but told me of a couple of instances from the past. Both she, and her family, have reported unusual events, including being followed by craft when driving down isolated roads. She has lived in both Australia and New Zealand, and like many other witnesses has seen normal looking 'humans' suddenly vanish into thin air.

As a child Glennys lived on a farm in Tasmania. She recalls a blond haired 'friend' who used to come and play with her, and tell her stories about Snow White and Alice in Wonderland. Glennys remembered being taken on a trip to a place she was told was 'Never Never Land.'

In 1964, when on a car trip, she was followed home by a strange craft, experienced some 'missing time' and recalls aliens in grey body suits with knobbly 'claw' fingers. After she was married Glennys lived on a farm in Greytown NZ, and they saw UFOs hovering close and near to the house. When in Masterton, a UFO landed in their back paddock. She also had sightings, one in particular near Wellington, at the same time Quenton Fogarty and the entire crew of his plane photographed strange lights in the sky.

When in New Zealand, and in contact with Bruce Cathie, Glennys was told she had cancer of the larynx. Six days after another encounter, the cancer was gone and she got her voice back.

Glennys has also spent time in Hawaii, the United States and South America. In September 1991, while in a plane above Arizona, she saw a round, disc-shaped UFO being pursued by five Stealth fighters. Other witnesses in the plane also witnessed the encounter.

Glennys has also reported other encounters with UFOs and tall, intelligent beings who look like us. These events often took place with her husband and others present. Her communication with the visitors has been mostly telepathic, and she also, like many other experiencers, has received warnings about coming earth changes.

THE DARK SIDE

George Adamski

In 1959, when George Adamski made a lecture tour of New Zealand, interference by powers unknown became quite evident.

It was in Christchurch, on the South Island, that problems started to occur. Five minutes before the projectionist was due to show the lecture slides, he demanded extra money, or he wouldn't work.

In Timaru the meeting was noisy, and there seemed to be an element in the audience that was trying to create trouble. Fred Dickeson was sure that the South Island meetings were deliberately being interrupted by 'outsiders' who had been 'bussed in'. Just before he was due to go on to Dunedin, the projector lens went missing, and a replacement had to be found.

The Dunedin meeting itself turned into a shambles. The hall lighting was wrong and the film had been incorrectly loaded into the projector. Precious time was wasted putting things right. Instead of writing their questions on a piece of paper at the break, some of the crowd started shouting out all at once. By the time order was restored it was nearly 10pm and they had to vacate the premises.

When Adamski was due to return to Auckland, to catch his flight to Sydney, and the Australian part of his tour, Fred Dickeson called at his Dunedin hotel to take him down to breakfast and then on to the airport. George was very shaken, looking startled and dazed. He said that two men in suits, had visited him previously that morning.

Just after 6am there had been a knock on the door, and George had opened it, wondering why Fred had come so early. Two men in the corridor had quickly pushed past him into the room, and cornered him between the bed and the dressing table. He could not reach the phone, which was on the other side of the bed.

They stood there for several seconds before one said; "You don't have your bodyguard with you now! It's a good thing you're leaving today, or we would have made it really difficult for you. We can't keep the crowds away from your meetings, but we can create disturbances like last night. You are lucky to get out of here alive - we don't want your sort here!" Their appearance and New Zealand accents left him in no doubt as to whom they were.

Fred called Jim, his Dunedin colleague. They and George agreed not to call the police, as any investigation would disrupt the scheduled flight plans to Australia for the lecture tour there. Adamski made both written and taped statements before he left.

Some, but not all New Zealand and other investigators, said they were 'threatened' by unknown, possibly government or security representatives.

Murray Stott

In September 1979, both the *'Daily Mirror'* and *'Sunday Times'* carried reports of how New Zealand investigator, Murray Stott said he was forced to flee Australia. He had been threatened after giving several lectures in Melbourne, and cancelled his planned research and lectures in Sydney.

The newspapers reported Murray as saying; *"I was walking back to the place I was staying in Sydney, when I noticed a Ford car parked a few houses down the road. Someone waved, and I thought they may be wanting directions. I walked over, and then someone jumped out the back, and said "Hop in, Murray".*

"There were three men in the car. They asked me about my lectures. I asked them who the hell they were, and if they didn't produce any identification, I would just get out. That's when the ginger-haired man in the front said; "We're telling you, for your own good, you had better leave". He said they did not want anyone talking about UFOs in Sydney. I tell you, the old heart was beating very fast when I got out."

Mr. Stott said all three men were respectfully dressed and groomed, and at first he had thought they were policemen; "I didn't take the number of the car. It's easy to be wise in hindsight, but I was pretty shook-up."

He told the *'Daily Mirror';* *"I am leaving Australia because although I had intended staying and continuing my research, I hardly think it is worth my life."*

Not to be deterred, in 1984, he wrote the book *'Aliens over the Antipodes'.*

Bruce Cathie

Whilst researching UFOs, and their connection to 'Earth Energy Grids', Bruce Cathie also suggested that these grids were crucial to our atomic bomb tests. In his book *'Harmonic 695'*, he mentions the reluctance of some experts to discuss this, and how he preferred to conduct his research individually, and had declined lucrative offers to work with other scientists.

He wrote that one scientist, who would not speak out, told him; "It's not for the public to know these things. It's not good for them."

(In his book, *'The Energy Grid'*, he wrote; *'I wonder; couldn't it be that the scientists already have the full explanation of UFOs – and for reasons not yet clear, are deliberately keeping the knowledge a jealously guarded secret within their own closed ranks'*

'Incredible as it may seem, this appears to be the truth. I have amassed a considerable amount of evidence which strongly suggests that scientists in a number of countries not only know a great deal about UFOs, they also know how to keep in contact with them. I believe that from such contacts, there has already been a considerable exchange of information.')

Cathie went on to say; *'As I dug in, closer to the truth of the UFOs and the power sources which they use, I was twice approached by a 'middle-man' who was interested only in finding whether or not I would stop my research for a price. When he found out that I was prepared to go on with my research, and publish at all costs, I was warned that unspecified 'strange things' would happen to me if I persisted. This is not a delusion of someone suffering from a persecution complex; it is perfectly true. A noted lawyer has the name, a record of the veiled threat and who made it.*

'I was able to give the middle-man his answer during a television interview. I let it be known I had taken a number of precautions – such having a number of manuscripts, charts, calculations, maps and other research data – placed in several safe spots, so that if anything untoward happened to me, the work would be carried on and eventually published anyway. I said that I was not afraid.'

Australian ufologist, Fred Stone, also wrote of the perceived threat to Bruce Cathie. In 1970, his book, *'Harmonic 33'*, was quite popular, and the publisher had arranged for him to give a lecture at an Adelaide UFO Convention which was being held over the Easter long weekend holiday.

Bruce seemed very enthusiastic, and travel and accommodation arrangements were made on his behalf. Suddenly, without explanation, he could not attend the Convention. Fred contacted the publisher, who advised that Bruce's life had been threatened, and the New Zealand police had advised him not to come because of the danger involved. (In a further development, Bruce himself told me of how, without explanation, his publisher had shredded all the copies of one of his books.)

Riley Crabb

Researcher, Riley Crabb, was a respected scientist who moved to Auckland in 1987. Peter Hassall wrote; *'soon after, he married pen-pal Phyllis Hall, Crabb said he feared for his life, after a couple of bungled murder attempts. He told an 'Auckland Sun' reporter that his home was bugged, and helicopters regularly spied on his house in the United States.'*

Suzy Hansen

In 1999, whilst a guest speaker at the International UFO Congress in Nevada, a 'Mexican' couple 'befriended' Suzy, and she innocently invited them into her room, instead of meeting them in a cafe. Their friendly demeanour soon turned sinister and menacing, they blocked her access to the door, and insisted she should return to New Zealand and cease talking publicly.

After they threatened the safety both Suzy and her sons, she managed to get past them and out of the room. Later, an ex-military 'person', also at the Congress, warned others that there were two 'agents' in the audience, posing as a Mexican couple.

CHAPTER THREE

The 1940s and 1950s

Lake Omapare 1942

During 1942 farmers in the Fiordland region of the South Island made several reports, ignored by both police and the authorities, of one or more silvery, saucer-shape craft cruising high over the mountains.

However, one night, at Lake Ompare, which was inland from the Bay of Islands, on the North Island, onlookers saw a large, silvery, glowing object which suddenly appeared as a flash from the centre of the water, and flew high into the sky, making a loud roaring sound as it headed northwards.

Christchurch, August 1944 (*Mrs. Church Case*)

I have always been interested in reports of modern-style unidentified objects before the alleged Roswell UFO crash of 1947:
Researcher Bruce Harding received a call from Mrs. Church in 1973, after a radio interview with Bryan Dickeson. Bruce investigated the details at length, and found no discrepancies in her testimony or disposition:

Mrs. Church, a senior theatre nursing sister at the local tuberculosis sanitorium, was sure it was August, because the Industries Fair was being held at the King Edward Barracks. She had the day off, and went instead for a walk around the Port Hills, east of the city and away from the crowds. She cut her walk short, as cloud was coming in fast, and didn't want to get lost.

"I decided to head back down through the low hilly slopes and scrub, to get the 4.30 p.m. tram home. There, sitting on a gentle slope, hidden from the road, was this upturned saucer.

"I was really curious, thinking 'What will they invent next?' I walked closer and stood staring for about eight to ten minutes. At first I thought it was some gimmick from the Industries Fair, but after I saw the 'little men' inside, (only four feet tall), I thought this must be some kind of Japanese device.

- Aluminium-coloured cap

- Blue light .

Mast-like projection -

Aluminium-coloured
"metal circle"

Light brown tiles with
a varnished, veneered,
type finish.

(Underneath of object - an absolutely
flat plane)

Door

"cockpit"

Occupant standing
in "window"

Occupant's
helmet

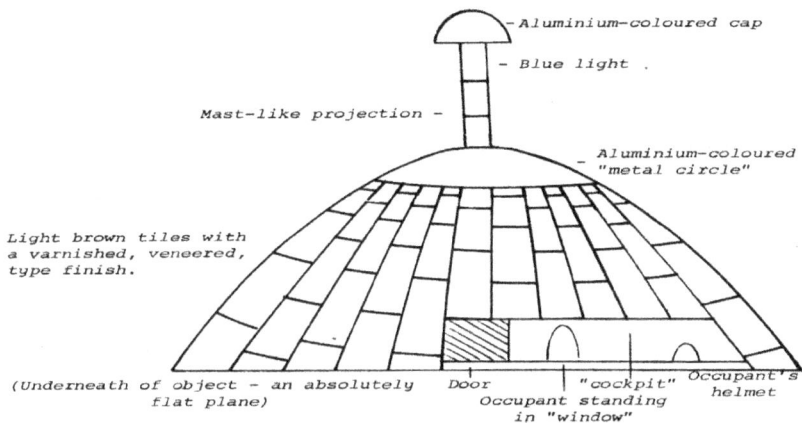

"The object was about eighteen–twenty feet across and eight–nine feet high, covered with light brown (almost wood grain-like) closely fitted vertical tiles, each about thirteen inches by ten inches. The base was dark brown and absolutely flat, with no lights and markings. There was a metal circle, (like dull aluminium) on top, somewhat like a protective cover, that fitted like a glove.

"On top was a two-foot high cylindrical projection, similar to a piece of four-inch pipe, with a mushroom shape aluminium colour cap.

"There were two little fellas, each inside a transparent casing, with a helmet on top. One was standing in the doorway–window, and I could see the top of another helmet in another window. A third was standing outside without a helmet, just a green-coloured being encased in a see-through oblong. He had quite a big head in proportion to his body; it would have been half his body height. The brief idea of fairies crossed my mind, but I thought; 'Don't be silly, they must be Japanese.' We hadn't even contemplated extraterrestrials in those days.

"The one outside was just standing there – I thought they were just watching the fair and the city below. The cloud came down and enveloped us, and I moved closer to talk to those people. I didn't even feel afraid, and hoped I might get a ride in their strange vehicle. I got quite close to him, only about twenty feet away, when I stood on something and made a slight noise.

"He saw me, and his helmet seemed to flip back on automatically. He drifted into the open doorway, which slid shut, and it looked like he was going into a cockpit.

"A blue light, started to shine steadily halfway up the mast on top, and I could hear a whirring noise, like a fan. The strange object rose vertically into the cloud, and I could see it climbing for a couple of minutes. I know this sounds silly, but as it took off, I wished I could have gone with it. I felt a sense of loss as it disappeared."

It appears that Mrs. Church caught her tram, so there was little missing time, if any. When she got back she asked one of the nursing sisters 'if there was a thing at the fair to take you for rides?' and she said; "No". Mrs. Church described an inexplicable sense of peace for the next week, and felt that there was an unseen presence in her room.

Later, whilst interviewing Mrs. Church, her husband mentioned an experience of his own, which had occurred at Greendale, on the North Island, sometime in 1919.

Dusk was falling as he returned from a rabbit shoot on his farm. He noticed a dull grey object, sitting in a creek bed some distance away. It was about fifteen feet across, elliptical in shape, and appeared to have a ramp protruding from its side. However, it was partially shielded from view by scrub, so after about thirty seconds, he started to move towards it, and as he did so, the object shot skywards, making a distinct whirring sound.

Taumarunui 1945

Mrs. Jolly, from *'The Hamilton Flying Saucer Investigation Group'.*, interviewed Mr. Bray, who in 1945 was a member of the RNZAF stationed at Rotorua. One midnight, whilst home on leave at Taumarunui, he observed a cigar-shaped object, showing red, yellow and orange alternating lights along its length. It left a definite trail as it passed overhead. About eight minutes later, another similar object appeared, flying the same north to south course.

Hamilton July 28th 1948

At 4.30pm, a woman with her daughter, who was home, on holidays from university, were upstairs on a sun-porch overlooking the Waikato River and facing the Te Aroha Mountains. Suddenly they saw a light approaching from the mountains, and as it came closer they realised it was a silver airship, which turned and followed the river's course. It appeared to be made of silver metal, shining in the sun, and was shaped like an inverted bowl. From the underpart came an intense light, so bright they could only liken it to a magnesium flare. They could not detect any wings or engine noise. They lost sight of it as it disappeared into the distance.

1951 February

In February 1951, there were a number of metallic, cigar-shaped objects sighted over a wide area of the South Island. Months later, a staff reporter from the *'Christchurch Star-Sun'* documented his own account; *'It was precisely at 3.46pm on November 21 that my wife and I watched an object over the foothills of the Southern Alps for seven minutes at least.*

'When we first saw it, it was gleaming brightly in the sun, and hanging motionless in the sky, probably at a height of more than 10,000ft, about four miles west of Coutts Island. It was cigar-shaped, and looked as though it might have been chromium plated, so intense was the light it reflected. At no stage did we hear any noise in the sky which could possibly have come from it.

'We watched for about three minutes whilst it hung motionless. Within another minute it began to move off quickly westward, towards and into the only cloudbank in sight, over the Southern Alps. As it moved, its shape did not change, but its size diminished with distance, and it appeared to emit two puffs of pink vapour....I am certain what we saw was not a airplane, a glider or a balloon.'

Auckland 1952

In his book, *'Harmonic 33'*, Bruce Cathie tells of an incident, one evening, near the local aero club at Mangere. The nearest Air Force Base was at Whenuapai. Several groups of witnesses saw a glaring white light, hovering motionless, at an altitude of less than 2,000ft, in the clear sky. Several hundred feet to the side, at the same elevation, was a smaller red light, which appeared to be rotating around the white one.

This continued for about ten minutes, before both lights slowly descended to about five hundred feet, where they remained motionless for another five minutes, after which they moved a short distance across the sky. The red light disappeared, and its white companion increased in brilliance and shot vertically upwards until it disappeared from sight.

Christchurch 1952

John Maybury, a New Zealand radio host, made a rather costly mistake in mid-1952. Years later, he told the '*Star Sports & Magazine*' how, for a couple of hours one morning, he faked a broadcast of pre-recorded fictitious eye witness reports of a UFO hovering over Hagley Park in Christchurch. A prominent local Anglican priest, with a lively sense of humour, had helped him with the scam, so it seemed a really great idea at the time. Unfortunately, it backfired.

He had got away with a few silly pranks in the past, and only two weeks earlier the Managing Director had told him to 'give radio a lift – inject more personality into your broadcasts!' John took him at his word. At 6am he had the fictitious UFO travelling across the countryside and hovering over the park. By 8.30am he had crashed the saucer and reported little green men running for the trees.

Thousands of people flocked to the park. Some came from twenty miles out of the city, causing one of the biggest traffic jams Christchurch had ever seen. The city was in an uproar, and the telephones 'went mad'. All the time John was sitting in his 3ZB radio studio, blithely broadcasting his ill-fated hoax.

Maybury was ordered off air, and banished to the radio station's programme department. He resigned, and didn't get another radio announcer job for another eighteen months.

Dunedin 28th October 1952

At 2.45am several residents were woken by a soft, high pitched, metallic noise. Mr. J. Burke, a pilot of eight years experience, watched a comparatively slow-moving cymbal-shaped disc for twenty minutes. It was steadily climbing higher into the sky, and was surrounded by a greenish, phosphorescent light, with a separate elongated section underneath.

6th December 1952

Between 8.45pm and 9.15pm, a pair of unidentified discs, one blue and one green, were reported by multiple witnesses on both the North and South Islands. Nearly all the reports were consistent, with witnesses saying that they could hear a slight 'hissing' sound, and the objects were heading in a southerly direction, at a speed calculated to be about 600 mph.

Hoaxes in 1952

Even in those early years, the newspapers were not immune from hoax reports, and researcher Peter Hassall, in his book, *'The New Zealand Files'*, tells of how one mean spirited hoaxer, Professor Scott, of Knox College, even fooled some of the sceptics. Twenty-five years later, the New Zealand Sceptics Society claimed that the professor had encouraged his students to make false reports during their school holidays. He even wrote out carefully devised scripts for them to follow. Of course, even if true, these pranks in no way accounted for all the sightings documented that year.

Taurmarunui 25th June 1954.

The *'New Zealand Herald'* and *'Auckland Star'* reported that at 8.30am a young child called to her mother, Mrs. Bell, to come and look at the 'flying saucer'. Once Mrs. Bell saw the strange object, she called out to Jack Mantell, the manager of Weir & Kenny's Mill.

Mantell stated; "I saw the object quite plainly. It was flying at about 25,000 feet, and it hovered in the sky when first seen. Then it suddenly vanished at terrific speed in a southerly direction. It was shaped like a large bowl, flattish and completely circular. I could distinguish what appeared to be two jets operating from one part of it."

Dunedin 24th August 1954

A long, dark, cigar-shaped object, with a bright orange light at the front, and a similar one at the rear, was seen by three nurses and a patient at Parkside Hospital. It was travelling at considerable speed, and only in view for a few minutes.

It was also seen by Mr. Pearcey and his wife. He said; "The object sighted by my wife and myself, at 9.30pm, was almost directly overhead when first seen, and travelled in a NNE direction, remaining visible for about a minute. The sky was clear, with no moon, and as the object passed overhead, I imagined I heard a low humming sound." Taieri Air force Base reported no aircraft flying at that time.

Earlier that day, at 2.48pm, a Taradale resident reported seeing a bright, silver disc from his orchard. It was at an altitude of several thousand feet when it passed overhead, and moved WNW. It appeared to be fairly large – clearly outlined for two minutes until it was obscured by cloud.

Nelson 9th September 1954

During 1954 there were multiple reports of green or blue coloured lights and unidentified objects traversing the New Zealand skies. Most were not observed up-close, so there were insufficient details to assist in any in-depth investigations.

'CSINZ' were quite excited when they were able to report their first authenticated photographs of an unidentified flying object. Mr. Gibbons, from Blenheim, had been holidaying at his parents' home in Nelson, when early in the morning, just after 2am, he went to the kitchen to get a glass of water.

Through the window he noticed some bright lights in the sky, and immediately got his camera and telescopic lens to snap his first photo of three disc-like objects, which were tilted in his direction. They were apparently hovering, in a close line formation, at an altitude of 300-400ft, over some mud flats about a quarter of a mile away. They were quite visible in the moonlit sky, and well below a patchy cloud base.

'Surrounding their dark centres was radiating a bluish-white illumination, which clearly outlined the 'inverted saucer' or 'convex' top-surface form. The outside pair, that were noticed, from the moment first sighted, to be wobbling like a top losing spin, suddenly stood on their edges, near vertically, and literally streaked upwards with terrific speed to disappear.

The centre, and remaining disc, now brightened up considerably, and this was when Mr. Gibbons managed the best and more distinct photograph. This disc now also began to wobble, turned flat, and just prior to departure, another photo was taken; the movement shows clearly on print. Mr. Gibbons took one more photo at the moment the disc began to rise vertically, but not as rapidly as the first pair. The former two had left so suddenly, the acceleration was not discernable – two white streaks being the only evidence of their upward path and departure. The objects had been in view for five minutes.'

At the same time, Mr. Alex Ingram, who lived about five miles away, noticed strange lights reflecting through his bedroom window, and investigated to see three illuminated 'moon-like' objects in the sky. At 11.20pm the following night, less than twenty-one hours later, Mr. Young, who lived only a mile-and-a-half away from Mr.Gibbon's parents' home, went out to the front gate and saw five illuminated discs hovering in the sky in the direction of the mud flats.

He gave a similar description of their flight characteristics, including wobble and departure. His young terrier dog was howling in apparent anguish from his kennel, and Mr. Young recalled that he had noticed the animal's similar behaviour previously, at about the same time Mr. Gibbons had seen the strange craft.

Leeston August 1955

Fred and Phyllis Dickeson documented the following report. *'At 4.45am, the first Sunday in August, two men were delivering milk when they noticed a strange orange light, with a shimmer or halo of lighter coloured light around it. It appeared in a gliding motion from a southerly to westerly direction.*

'The town of Leeston has a network of about one square mile of street lights, and when the object crossed over the area, the lights seemed as though they had a master switch, and were switched off in areas as the object passed. When it had passed these areas, they appeared as though switched on again. There was no noise and no swish. It climbed to 2-3,000ft, stopped, hovered in a swaying fashion – side to side. It took off in a vertical rise and went out of sight.

'Two electric clocks, in direct line of flight, went off at 4.45am. The Matron, at 6am asked the milkmen if there had been a power outage earlier on in the morning, as the power had gone off in the hospital for a few seconds.'

Gisborne 1956

In 1956, a New Zealand freight train was about ten kilometres south of Gisborne, on the east coast of the North Island. They were running behind time, and after rounding a bend, speeded up.

Ahead of them, at a height of about five hundred feet, and to the right of the track, were four large, circular balls of intense white light. Each one was 'the size of a small room', and they were flying in formation, with one ahead, two abreast and one astern. They seemed to be rising, as if to fly above a hill, and cross the bay to Gisborne. Suddenly, they changed direction, shot off high in the air, and passed over the back of the train.

In 1958, another locomotive crew were frightened by four similar unidentified objects which stalked their train for a considerable period of time.

Waiomo Valley 1956

Sometimes we cannot be sure if the injuries to a witness were deliberate or inadvertent. In '*UFOs – Now and Then*', I wrote about the 1956 case of sixteen-year-old Shayne Hura.

Early one morning he was cycling to his part-time job at a bakery in the Waiomo Valley. He was suddenly enveloped by a strange fog, and when it lifted, he saw a bright green, cigar-shaped object, with a fiery exhaust, climbing vertically into the sky.

Two days later, whilst traversing the same route, he was cycling past Sharpe's Quarry when he noticed a bright ball of solid light, about sixty centimetres in diameter, up beside the cliff face. He watched for a short time before continuing on his way, and he suddenly noticed that the strange object had risen out of the quarry, and was keeping pace with him.

That was the last he remembered, and said that he must have blacked out. The baker arrived to find Shayne collapsed at the bakery door, covered in blood and crying for help. Some of his teeth were missing, his nose was pierced, and his lip was torn away. His boss took him to hospital, and later found Shayne's bicycle in a creek seven kilometres away. The frame was bent, and the front wheel buckled, but police could find no evidence of any collision with a car.

Whilst Shayne recovered, he surprisingly felt the experience had changed his life for the better. Although he had no memory of the time he was 'blacked-out', he developed certain 'psychic' abilities, and once recovered in a Darwin hospital after 'dying' from a venomous snake bite.

Near Waikumete 10th June 1956

Harold Fulton documented a report from 10th June, when at about 9.30pm, one cold, wet night, whilst walking down the street, Brian Lovelock saw a strange object, hovering about 200ft above the ground. It resembled an upside-down saucer, with a ball-shaped top, and was emanating a blue-white light which alternatively dimmed and brightened. Without warning, it suddenly sped straight up into the sky, and disappeared.

Hamilton 6th August 1956

'CSI' published an account from a witness who, at 4.10pm., was driving from Hamilton to Taumarunui and saw the sun reflecting off a round, silvery object in the sky. It was a perfectly clear-cut sphere or disc, at an altitude of approximately 3,000ft. Suddenly, it rose rapidly, and he lost sight of it when it passed behind a cloud. Whilst he had never previously believed in 'flying saucers', he commented that nothing man made could climb at that rate of acceleration.

Auckland 16th September 1956

At 8pm., eleven amateur astronomers were gathered to study Mars, which was on a closer than usual approach to Earth. They also noticed a long, glowing, cigar-shaped form, the light from which seemed to be passing through all the colours of the spectrum. Through their telescope, they were startled to see three similar disc-shaped forms, which emerged and moved away from the larger object, and hovered in a group before moving off.

After a short period, they returned and merged back into the larger object, which then shot off into space, and was lost from view.

Hamilton 20th September 1956

'CSI' published the following report in their Quarterly Journal; *'Southwell boys and masters won't forget the 20th September, maybe for some time to come. At approximately 4pm on that date, a brilliant white object, slightly larger than the moon, held their undivided attention. Mr. Parry, one of the masters, forwarded the report.'*

He said the object was due north, at an altitude of three to four thousand feet. It was a perfect disc, dazzling white in colour, with no apparent markings, motion or spinning. For over a minute, three masters and fifty boys watched as it hovered, before suddenly moving away to the north, at remarkable speed until it was lost from sight. Shortly after, a Hamilton housewife, who was taking the washing off the line, spotted a brilliant white, dome shaped object, as large or larger than the full moon. She said it was travelling north, at a moderate speed, and emitting flashing beams of light.

Ngaruawahia 6th October 1956

Frank Duggan, a cafe proprietor, and his wife were woken at 4.10am by a bright light shining through their bedroom window, and they could see, in the sky outside, something similar to a brilliantly lit orange disc or saucer, but only longer, which was on its edge.

They watched for fifteen minutes as it hovered. Suddenly it seemed to start spinning, made a 'whirring' noise, and moved in a westerly direction, dropping and rising in sharp, swift movements. As it gained in altitude, they finally lost sight of it,

Waipukurau, 26–27 November 1956

On the night of 26-27 November residents reported unusual activity in the skies above.
At Hatuma, twelve miles from Waipukurau, local farmer Mr. Kibblewhite, woke at 2.10 a.m. on the 27th November, with a cramp in his knee, and got out of bed to walk around and ease off the pain. He was about to get back into bed, when a flash of light reflected on the mirror in front of him. He turned around, thinking someone was outside shining a torch through the open window.

As he looked out he saw a very bright bluish- silver colour beam, coming from a round object, high in the sky. The beam was round, like a pipe, about twelve to eighteen inches through, with clear cut edges. There was no diffusion of light from it, and it was so dense he could not see through it. It cut out after a few seconds. The object remained for a few seconds more, before making a sideways-rotating movement and vanishing.

Mr. Kibblewhite's report was initially met with scepticism. However, another resident, Mr. Reehal of Puketapu (75 kilometres northeast of Hatuma) saw exactly the same sort of beam over two hours earlier at 11.30 p.m. on 26th November. It had woken him when it shone into his room. He had gone out onto the veranda, and watched as it shone down through poplar trees.

Kaponga, late 1956
On 5th September, Mr Thomson, a Kaponga farmer, had been treating a sick animal, and at 1.30am went out to check that the injections he had administered earlier that night were taking effect. As he was walking down the property, he heard a hissing noise, increasing in intensity. Above him was a white light, followed by a blue one.

He could make out a huge white aircraft, unlike anything he had seen before, travelling across the sky at a surprising speed, perhaps 300-400 miles per hour, and an altitude of about 1,500 feet. He estimated it was about sixty feet long and thirty feet wide, with a glass-type dome, from which a blue light emanated. It had a small turret-like glass nose, which bulged out in front and from which the white light came. It had delta-like rounded wings, and a tapering tail which he could not see very well.

Haurakai Gulf 28th April 1957

At 4.30pm, Ron Matheson was navigating a fishing boat, the *'Rosa'*, off Port Charles on the Coramandel Coast. He held a third engineers certificate, and was delivering the boat from Tauranga to its owner in Auckland.

When he neared Cape Colville, he noticed an irregular smoke trail from behind Channel Island. As he passed the island, he realised the smoke was coming from a greyish, oval shape disc, out over the Haurakai Gulf. It was fairly narrow, and resembled two saucers, face to face together, with upper and lower portions similarly curved. Smoke was pouring from its sides. He watched for at least twenty minutes as it moved on an irregular, ever changing course.

He estimated it to be of an enormous size, perhaps several hundred feet in diameter, and travelling at an amazing speed. It was obviously controlled by something or somebody, and just before it flew off, it levelled out, then moved away, very rapidly, in horizontal flight towards and over the mainland.

Auckland June 24th 1957

A little after10am, John Bryce, a telegram dispatcher, spotted a bright silvery disc, stationary in the sky, over Devonport. It was clearly defined, and oval in shape. Suddenly it appeared to speed away, and ascend steeply into the sky until it was lost from sight.

Only four days later, on 28th June, four men working on an elevated machine in Christchurch, saw what they believed to be a flying saucer. At about 10.45am, they saw an aluminium disc which 'came at them', flying on its side with the sun gleaming on it. It appeared to hover for a while, and then flattened out before speeding off and disappearing in the west.

According to the business man, on whose shop they were working, he was certain the report was genuine. "The look in their eyes bore this out," he said.

Waikato 7th November 1957

'CSINZ' Reported that some residents of Paeroa saw a strange pink object moving in the south-western sky from about 10.40 to 10.50pm. It was flying slowly from the west until it eventually disappeared over the horizon. The same night, the Canberra Mt. Stromlo Observatory tracked a similar unknown object, which was moving much slower than the then first Russian satellite.

Mount Teranaki 7th June 1958

Three young couples, plus other witnesses, were about to leave a residence where they had been spending the evening, when they spotted a round, ground-based, dark-red glow around the base of Mount Teranaki (aka Mt. Egmont), about eight miles away.

The ground glare was radiating up into the sky, and after they had watched for about ten minutes, debating what it might be, a large white oval object rose quickly, but flatly from the centre of the red glow. It paused momentarily, then rapidly climbed steeply away, passing over their heads. At a height of about three to four thousand feet if paused briefly, then shot vertically into the sky, disappearing within a few seconds.

Some fifteen minutes later, all signs of the red ground-glow had vanished, however the three young men later decided to investigate further. Armed with survey maps and compasses, and accompanied by a *'CSI'* investigator, who had also received a report of strange lights that night, their magnetic compasses and radio started to malfunction when they reached the area where the red glow had been seen.

Blenheim, 13th July 1959 (*Mrs. Moreland Case*)
One of the most-reported close encounter cases from New Zealand is the sighting by Eileen Moreland, and I thank Bryan Dickeson for his research notes on this case.
After the incident, many reporters and media accounts were incorrect in their details, so in order to present the accurate details, this is Mrs. Moreland's letter to investigator Henk Hinfelaar.

'At about 5.30am, on the morning of July 13th 1959, I was going out across the paddock to bring in the cows for milking, after having switched on the light in the shed. The morning was very cold, with a thick cloud which has been roughly estimated at about 2,000 feet.

'I was about half-way across the paddock, when I noticed an odd green glow in the clouds directly above me. I stopped to look at it, thinking that it couldn't be the moon, (anyway, it was in the wrong place), when suddenly two green lights, like large 'eyes' appeared through the cloud. The ground was illuminated with this sickly green light, and when I looked down at myself, I too was bathed in this light. I immediately thought; "I shouldn't be here", and I bolted for the pines which border the paddock. I could see the cows plainly in the light, and I ran among them and stood against a tree.

'When I turned round, the saucer was about fifty feet from the ground and slowly descending. There were two rows of jet-like flames, sprouting from two bands at the top and bottom of the 'fuselage'. These were of a brilliant orange, fading off to yellow, and made a faint hissing noise. At about 15ft from the ground, it abruptly halted and became motionless, just hanging there. At once the jets shut off and reappeared at an angle; each had a band that began to whirl at a high speed, with little or no 'revving' up. This was accompanied by a faint humming sound.

'I then noticed that the ship was occupied, and I am afraid I was scared stiff. The clear plexiglass or Perspex, (or whatever the material was), cabin was lit with a pure white light, though I couldn't see the source of the light. The two men were seated one behind the other, at more than an arm's length apart. They were dressed in almost skin-tight suits of some shiny material like aluminium foil which wrinkled with each moment and deflected little points of light. The rear man suddenly stood up and leaned forward on his hands, and appeared to be looking down at something between them. I could see a reflection of a flickering light in front of him, but could not see what it was. I did not get a glimpse of their features as the huge helmets which took in from shoulder to shoulder, were opaque and silver like the suit. The man then sank back in his seat, the ship tilted at a slight angle, the bands of jets stopped whirling, and the jets appeared as when descending, and with a mighty 'whoosh' of air it rose vertically, still at the slight angle, and vanished into the cloud at tremendous speed, accompanied by a high pitch whine. I never thought anything could move at such a speed, it was unbelievable.

'A moment or two later, the atmosphere became noticeably warm, and there was a strange smell of 'hot pepper'. After a moment or two, I pulled myself together, as it were, collected the cows, which had not been in the least bit alarmed at the strange object, and drove them to the yard. As I did so, I heard the town clock chime a quarter to six, so the visit could not have been more than two to three minutes, although it seemed ages.

'I milked as usual, put the milk out at the gate, and then flew inside with my story. Everyone was soon awake. My husband believed me, and told me to ring the police. I was hesitant at first, saying; "Who is going to believe I saw such a thing?" However, I did ring, and they were mightily interested. My husband, who is a member of the R.N.Z.A.F. at Woodbourne, notified the authorities there, who, far from scoffing at the story, took it very seriously, as I have since found out. However, they do believe it, and that is the main thing as far as I am concerned, though I have vowed never to say a word if 50 land in my paddock at once. I don't think it's worth it, I couldn't go through all that again. You may think I am talking in riddles, I guess, but it is all a riddle to me.'

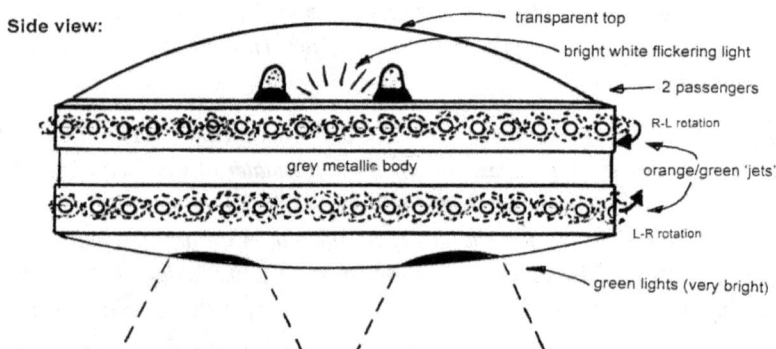

Side view:

transparent top
bright white flickering light
2 passengers
R-L rotation
grey metallic body
orange/green 'jets'
L-R rotation
green lights (very bright)

In a later tape-recorded interview with investigator Reg Gledhill, a few more details came out. The craft was apparently about twenty-five feet wide and five feet high, and it was hovering just over some ten-fifteen feet peach trees.

The same morning, three miles east of Mrs. Moreland's location at Blenheim, Mr. Holdaway had got up, sometime between 4.30 and 5am., to get a glass of water, and saw a bright light shining through the window. It appeared to be a whitish/orange colour, became brighter until it reached a high intensity, and gradually faded away, without any accompanying sound.

Researchers from the *'Blenheim UFO Club'* later claimed that at the same time as Mrs. Moreland's sighting, four different drivers had sighted a similar object, and that morning, a Blenheim farmer had seen an 'unforgettable' green light, which lit up his whole house.

Colin Amery, another N.Z. researcher, later wrote that the wife of a wing Commander at the nearby Air Force Base heard, at 5.45am, what she thought was a jet aircraft pass overhead; *'Her husband checked it out, when he went to work, but there were no jets in the air at that time. This evidence was withheld from the inquiry, which was held behind closed doors – the results were never made public. I have since heard of several other people who also witnessed the sighting. I am sure that since then the government has been aware, at very high levels, of just what is going on.'*

In December 1959, Mrs. Moreland wrote again to researcher Henk Hinfelaar. In it were some interesting comments; *'At the present, I am sorry that I am unable to disclose the name of the V.I.P. responsible for the enquiry, as there is at present 'Security' on the subject. I wonder if I may be a little more open with you, but would you mind respecting my confidence, and refrain in further correspondence, from referring to what I am about to say.*

'There is a great more to the story than has ever got out, (and for my part will remain undisclosed), so there is a deep silence on the subject. Only a handful know the full details, and as my husband is also a member of the R.N.Z.A.F. and holds a responsible position, you will realise the seriousness should names be broadcast. This is very confusing to you, I know, but believe me, I am in earnest.'

The incident attracted a lot of attention, and in another letter to Mr. Steeds, she bemoaned the queer stories and distortion of facts that had been published. She then disclosed; *'In strictest confidence, I had a dreadful time at the hands of higher authorities, and although they are now convinced my story is quite true, as I came through the ghastly interrogation and noise tests successfully, I couldn't go through all that again. You will appreciate the fact that no-one else knows the above, I know. I don't blame them for not being quite sure I was not 'pulling someone's leg' for the fun of it, but all the same. Flying saucers are 'off' as far as I am concerned.'*

In another letter to a Mr. Bennett, she mentioned how one investigator had been taunting her, calling her a liar. She felt that this was an attempt to get her to release more details. She wrote; *'He wrote me one or two quite insulting letters, hoping that I would be stung into leaping to my own defence by letting out information that I have been forbidden to divulge. I can prove the truth of my experience, but have been forbidden to do so by those greater than I, so of course, as Queen and country count, I, of course, keep quiet, and let him carry on calling me what he will. He'll get tired of it long before I will.'*

After the extensive publicity Mrs. Moreland was plagued by hordes of inquisitive sightseers, who wandered all over the property, leaving gates open, upsetting the cows and generally creating such a nuisance that she and her husband said that if either of them ever saw another object they would prefer to 'shut-up' about it. In later years, the couple divorced, and Mrs. Moreland remarried and moved to Rotorua.

Years later Mrs. Moreland received a letter from Charles Brew, who claimed a similar incident in Moe, Vic. Australia, on 15th February 1962. In it, he mentioned having a severe headache afterwards.

In another letter to Hinfelaar, in March 1967, Mrs. Moreland confirmed that after the incident she also had a terrible headache, which lasted for several days. *'My eyes were also affected, and I have a permanent film over them as if I were looking through slightly smoked glass. I have, since that experience, had to wear glasses during the day, something I never had to do prior to that occasion...I have to ask you, of course, to treat the matter of my eyes as confidential. This is not to get out for Security reasons. There is other I could tell you, but that must wait until such time we meet.'*

Although she did not report other detrimental side effects at the time, Bryan Dickeson investigated the occurrence in depth, and reported the following; *'Several days after the incident, Mrs. Moreland's hands began to swell, and get puffy. The backs of her hands developed small pustules, which oozed watery liquid when she scratched them. Her doctor unsuccessfully tried every hand cream he knew, but they finally stopped after about six months. Her wedding ring became painfully tight, and had to be cut off. Brown pigmented areas developed on her face, and she referred these conditions to her doctor. The swelling in her hands gradually subsided, but the brown patches on her face persisted considerably longer. The last blotch over her right eyebrow washed off some six years later.*

'Later on, the row of fruit trees, where the UFO had hovered, died, and had to be pulled out. However, the grass in the vicinity grew at a much faster rate, and was several times taller and much greener than grass elsewhere in the paddock.'

Bryan also noted; *'Mrs. Moreland was also interviewed by Air Force personnel who visited the farm. They told her they found higher than normal levels of background radiation where the object had been seen.'*

Wanganui 3rd November 1959

Two businessmen reported seeing a strange object, at 11.30am, over the trees in the Woodlands district. It was a disc, with a dome on top, and a smaller dome underneath. It suddenly turned on its side, and moved away at tremendous speed.

Two days later, at 11.30pm, one of the men was followed along the road by a similar object. When he got home, his wife and daughter also saw the strange craft.

Invercargill 8th December 1959

The *'Taranaki Daily News'* told of dozens of people who watched a strange object in the sky over Invercargill shortly after midnight. *'An Invercargill insurance agent said he was travelling down Elles Road South when he noticed crowds of children pointing to the sky. He did not take much notice until he saw housewives and shopkeepers coming out to have a look.*

'Stopping his car, the insurance agent saw what he described as an object much bigger than a DC-3 aircraft. It was longer by far, and looked – "just like a saucer looks when placed upside down on a table, only it was the same thickness all along." It was hovering at about 1,000ft below cloud level.'

One witness, who was an amateur astronomer, told the Invercargill UFO Group leader, that he had watched the object for about three minutes, and estimated it to be over 1,200ft long and with a diameter of nearly 140ft.

CHAPTER FOUR

The 1960s

By the beginning of the 1960s, some members of the press were well and truly fed up with all the reports of UFOs. In February 1965, The Dickesons wrote the following in their *'SATCU'* Newsletter'

'The following was probably published in the 4th February 'Southland Times', in order to throw cold water on the recent saucer sightings in New Zealand; it is amusing, but informative, as many a true word is spoken in jest.

'Mystery Object Season Has Opened'

'The season for Unidentified Flying Objects seems to be a little early this year. The season should begin about September, and carry through to about January – or so the records show.

'In November 1955, there was a week in which no-one picking up a newspaper could fail to see a story about unidentified flying objects. This particular spate was started when a N.A.C. pilot found something flying alongside his aircraft.

'Going back to 1909, when the 'phantom airship' was doing the rounds, the spate for that season began in Britain. It went from there to Dunedin, and then to Auckland.

'It seems that New Zealand has another 'season' of sightings on its hands. A sighting in Christchurch on Monday, many sightings on Wednesday, and now one in Invercargill. These sightings are quite ordinary – especially when one sits back and sifts through newspaper accounts of sightings from years back. It may well be a lifetime job to go back through the last fifteen years. In that time there have been about one hundred reported sightings.

'In Wyndham, in 1953, there were 'flying trees' – complete with roots! At about 2,000 feet, they appeared to be six or eight feet long.

'At Gore, a huge light appeared four nights later. This one was a 'heavenly body' – it had a 'halo'. A year later, someone found a 'football that turned sharply'. Lumsden, not to be outdone, found a lighted football about 200ft long. One morning, the same year, a 'tennis ball', which moved with the speed of a

'tracer bullet' shot over Invercargill. Earlier that year, Invercargill had something round that hissed as it went by.

'These were nothing on the 1909 sighting over Otago and Southland'. It was shaped like a boat with a flat top, speeding along at something like 30mph, its body resembling 'something like that of a whale'.

'Many brands of cigars are found too. Someone with exceptional eyesight found 'a white cigar-shaped object, flat along the bottom and curved at the top', at ten o'clock at night. Another saw a pulsing cigar over Auckland. It was about 10.000ft and made a 'half-whoosh'.

'Next in popularity were the saucers. They come in all shapes and sizes, even upside down! There are baby saucers, which appear at 1,500ft, about three feet in diameter, or they may have a rocking motion. One upturned saucer had a bell-shaped dome which flickered.

'If discs can be called saucers, they can appear accompanied by sparks, in giant sizes. And in any colour one likes to order. Discs can also hiss. Someone in Omaru found the answer to a lonely saucer. He found a 'flying teacup'. This one was inverted, and complete with mast.

'The objects are known to have revolving lights about them, and travel in formations at speeds up to 1,000 miles per hour. Some revolve on an apex – this, apparently, is a Northland variety.

'Some objects have three or four lighted windows. They have been known to leave a vapour trail. One man in New Plymouth, who said that he had 'two perfectly good eyes', saw something at 10pm that had numerous turrets, a tapered tail, and measured seventy feet by thirty feet. It was flying at 1,500ft..

'Others can go in circles, zig-zag, or stay still for a couple of hours. Many views have been expressed about such flying objects. Some years ago, Mr. W. Anderson, a Fellow of the 'Royal Astronomical Society', said that they were 'natural phenomena'.

Kevin O'Brien walked into the Dominion newspaper office in Wellington once, and said that flying saucers were propelled by electro-magnetic motors, and that they did not come from anywhere on earth. If they landed in a school field, (for he was aged twelve), there would be no need to panic – 'we would just have to settle things peaceably'.'

The article went on to say that many sightings had turned out to be satellites or meteorites, however life could be made difficult, and subject to ridicule for pilots who made reports.

Fred Dickeson made public his thoughts about this article when he wrote; *'As usual, the attempt to cover-up is rather pathetic. People KNOW what they see, they are not dim-wits, but the only way to explain something is to liken it to a well known object which everyone knows, hence the varied descriptions.'*

In spite of the media scepticism, genuine reports still came flooding in.

Rotorua early February 1960

Stan Downard, one of the Rotorua Group investigators, interviewed M. Tu, a Maori bus driver, who was travelling one night with two passengers, as they returned from the Waitangi Celebration, which had been held up north.

They spotted an unusual 'searchlight' in the sky, but when they reached the top of a plateau, it was seen to be oval, and hovering about sixty feet above the ground, and slightly higher than a row of pine trees in a neighbouring paddock. It was about 230 feet away from the road. Mr. Tu stopped the bus, and he and his passengers got out to get a better look.

The strange, silent object, estimated to be about sixty feet in diameter, was moving in a slow pendulum-like manner, and had a broad cone of light emanating from underneath. It illuminated the fields, fences and cattle below.

Another car came along, and they all watched for a few minutes, when a feeling of apprehension overtook them, and they decided to 'get out quick'. Upon proceeding on their journey, the object appeared to keep pace with them for about a mile, before shooting off at high speed.

Wairau Valley March 1960

In March 1960 Mrs. N. was lying in bed, which was close to the window at the front of her house, twenty miles down the Wairau Valley. At about 11.30pm, glow of green light seemed to come from behind her home, and within a short time it lit up the entire bedroom. She got up, looked through the window, and was astounded to see an object over the house, and slightly to one side.

It was a large, circular shaped disc, made of silvery metal, and about thirty-five feet in diameter. At the centre was a 'sort of glowing canopy', with a diameter of about ten feet, and shining a strong blue-green light. It was travelling slowly and silently, at about thirty miles per hour.

Mrs N. watched in amazement. The craft came within fifty feet of her window, level with the tops of some young pine trees, which were only about thirty feet high.

What was unusual about this sighting was that the object was travelling on edge, and looked like a huge coin rolling on its rim, slowly revolving in the direction of its travel. It slowly passed out of sight, over a nearby hill, and the glow finally receded.

Apparently the strange craft left no traces behind, the animals did not appear to be affected, and there were no scorch marks on the ground. Mrs N. was not really interested in UFOs, and thinking people would treat it as a joke, it was only by chance she mentioned it to one of the researchers.

Invercargill 19th September 1960

The *'Wanganui Herald'* reported how two women and a man, for about an hour, watched a large saucer-shaped object giving off a very bright light. At first, it was seen at a distance in the west, where it appeared as three lights. As it came closer, the three lights seemed to merge into one. They thought it was at a height of about 1,500ft.

One woman said; "It was like a saucer – it seemed to have a bowl underneath. It was just like the spaceships in my children's comics." There were no aircraft in the sky at the time.

Tairua Jan/Feb 1961

'NZSSRG' spoke to a Coromandel Peninsular farmer, who, one night, along with his family, saw a bright disc circle their house, then swoop down over another house, on a lower level, before 'making off'.

The next day they went to their neighbour's home, but before they could say anything, they were greeted with; "Did you see that flying saucer swoop over our house last night?"

That same man related an experience which had occurred about eighteen months earlier; *'He had been working on his tractor, and had stopped for a rest, when he noticed what he thought at first to be an aircraft, flying near some rough hills.*

'As the object came below the hilltops, however, it was not light reflections which caught his eye, but that the object glowed. It came down between the hills and landed in what appeared to be a small clearing. Its appearance was spherical. After a short period, he saw movement around the object, and 'they' seemed to put something out like a 'ground marker', after which the object looked as though it was partly covered.

'He watched for about an hour, then went to his house to find his binoculars, but being unable to locate them, returned to the spot and continued to observe the object until it finally rose up, wavered, and shot away.'

He estimated he had been scrutinising it for about two-and-a-half hours, and noted that the country around the area was very rough, and it would have taken him at least an hour-and-a-half to get to the spot where the object had landed.

Auckland 18th February 1962

Just after midday, and Mr. and Mrs. Hooper, of Brown's Bay, were startled when their three children, and two playmates, raced into the house and told them to come and look at something outside in the sky. They joined the children, and later reported: "It was a beautiful clear blue sky, with hardly any clouds to be seen, and this object, which was slightly to the north of directly overhead, shone with the brightness of a star.

"It appeared to be very high, and about the size of a threepence, held at arm's length. It remained stationery, and there was no sound whatsoever. It remained like that for approximately two or three minutes, then slowly turned over. This was plainly seen – the object glinted as the sun caught it turning, and as the underside came into view, it became duller, in fact opaque, like smoke, but at the same time it was easier to see that the object was distinctly round.

"As we watched, it seemed to go straight up, higher and higher until it faded completely from view, in a matter of seconds. We have never witnessed anything of the like before, and we are of the opinion that it was not a balloon, aeroplane or meteor." *(NZSSRG)*

Waihi 17th April 1962

Investigator Colin Lambert submitted the following report; *'At approximately 7.45am, four-year-old Diane, daughter of Waihi farmer Mr. Archer, remarked to her mother; "That must be the last star going to bed."*

'Mother, cutting the lunches for the older children, suddenly realised her daughter should not be able to see a star in daylight, and decided to investigate. On opening the back door, she was amazed to see a clear-cut, round, silvery disc, which she described as a 'shiny half crown', cruising along fairly low above the hills. It was travelling from N.W. to S.E., and remained in view for two to three minutes before disappearing from her vision behind some trees.

Gisborne 29th April 1962

'NZSSR' documented a report from two miles east of the city, when at 10.35pm, a mother along with her two teenage daughters, observed a bright light, hovering in the sky. They said; "The size appeared fairly large, as the outline of the object, as well as the dome, were clearly discernable. Portholes could be seen, due to the light shining from them, and when the craft moved, they lit up with a bright, glowing orange colour.'

The craft descended to the slopes of a hilltop, but the witnesses were not sure if it hovered very close to the ground, or actually landed. It remained stationary for approximately ten minutes, and then rose slowly to disappear over the undulating hills.

9th July 1962

'The New Zealand Herald' reported that just after 9pm, a deep red 'aurora' , striped with jets of white light, swept in a broad band over the New Zealand sky. If residents thought it was some form of extraterrestrial activity, they were wrong. Four thousand miles away, to the north in the Pacific, a U.S. task force had exploded a test nuclear weapon over Johnston Island. Some effects were also seen by scientists based in the Antarctic.

This provoked an outcry, and general concern by many people in New Zealand.

Antarctica Early July 1962

To the south of the country lies the Antarctica, where New Zealand had its remote Cape Hallett Station. Late one evening, from 11.10pm to 11.13pm, scientific leader, C. Taylor, and seven of the station crew, saw and photographed a strange object, travelling from southwest to northeast in the sky.

It had three yellowish-white lights, the centre light being mid-way between the other two. When in the northern sky, the strange craft emitted a brilliant flash of white light. Mr. Taylor, having ruled out a stray weather balloon, stated; "I don't know what it was. It was too slow for a meteorite, and too fast for a satellite."

Tokoroa 1963

In those years it was easy for children to be silenced, or even not believed. In 1988, researcher John Pinkney spoke to Carol MacKenzie, who in 1963, was a pupil in a school at Tokoroa in New Zealand.

She was only eleven at the time, and at lunchtime, was playing in a field behind the school. Five metallic, domed and 'leaden-coloured' UFOs, each about six metres in diameter, hovered overhead. She and her schoolmates watched as they came, in formation, closer in the sky. They stopped for a moment before flashing away over the hills.

That night, when she told her parents, all she got was condescending smiles, and despite there being other reports, and even photographs on the front page of the local newspaper the next day, countless so called 'experts' claimed that what they had seen was all in their imaginations!

Invercargill 27th February 1963

'*NZSATCU*' reported that an Invercargill man woke his family at 2.30am after he saw, through his bedroom window, a strange object in the sky.

He leapt out of bed, and went to a window in the front of the house, where he saw three, silver-grey, round objects flying below the clouds. They seemed to be in formation, with the centre object ducking and diving about. They were moving from north to south-west, at a fairly low altitude, and were spinning in a way no aircraft could have.

Invercargill 14th December 1963

It was 5am when a Woodend resident was wakened by what sounded like a lorry, travelling at high speed. Upon looking out the window, he was startled to see a dome-shaped object rushing by at about sixty to one hundred feet above the ground. It was on a straight, level trajectory, and shedding a blue light. Two other people in the house were also wakened by the noise, but due to the objects speed, it had disappeared before they could join the witness at the window.

Auckland 28th December 1964

'*NZSSRG*' interviewed two teenage girls and their mother after a saucer-shaped craft was seen over Auckland Domain at 9pm. It was rotating, and looked like two silvery saucers joined together, with a 'turret' or 'control room' at the top. Red and white lights were visible around the central rim, with a larger green light at the top of the 'turret'.

It hovered at an altitude of about fifty feet, above the trees, and was clearly visible to the witnesses, who were only sixty yards away.

Auckland 17th January 1965

Henk Hinfellar's files told of Vainney Turner, who worked a Saturday night shift in a city coffee lounge. It was 4.15am by the time she got home, and she had to let the dog out for a couple of minutes before going to bed. Vainney looked up into the sky, and saw a circle of rotating, bright yellowish-white, round lights.

Although she couldn't see any finer details of the object, she thought it was about forty feet in diameter, about thirty feet away, with an altitude of only fifty feet. She became frightened, and ran inside to wake her mother, but by the time they both came out again, it had gone.

South New Brighton – Christchurch – February 1965

This report is from the personal notes of Bryan Dickeson, who investigated this report some two-and-a-half years later.

'At that time, Cliff W. (then aged 18), was between jobs, and minding house for a friend in the southern part of Rockinghorse Road, New Brighton. Early that evening he took his host's dog for a walk on the nearby New Brighton beach, to get out of the house. It was mid-week, during late summer. The days were still very warm, not many people were about, (as children had recently gone back to school), and the beach was deserted.

'....The dog got a bit 'skitterish' when they neared some sand dunes. On looking more carefully, Cliff noticed a large metallic disc, nestled in a depression, between some larger dunes, amongst some tall clumps of marram grass.

'He moved closer to get a better look – (to within about twelve yards). The disc was a little under twenty feet across, and over three feet high...The joined-together top and bottom sections were identical, and made of a light grey metal – like aluminium – very smooth and polished, but not reflective. No seams or rivets were visible, and there was a yellowish light around the whole object. The glow was unusual, making the disc look slightly 'blurred' up close.

'It took him a while to realise that the glow started faintly about five to seven inches from the metal surface, and got more intense nearer to the metal. But then the glow stopped completely about half an inch from the surface – there was a thin glow-free air layer immediately around the disc. The disc was rounded, with about a quarter of an inch diameter cross-section, as if the metal was 'folded', and not sharp.

'The disc also radiated some warmth – it got slightly warmer as you got closer. There was a low humming noise coming from the object, but otherwise the area seemed very quiet, 'unusually quiet', and very sheltered from any breeze or the sea.

'After looking at the object for a minute or two, he sat down on the sand, facing the disc, with his elbows on his knees. He picked up a small piece of driftwood from the sand and lobbed it at the disc. The driftwood fell towards the top of the disc, but 'slowed down' as it neared the metal surface and rolled off, back onto the sand, 'a bit like water from a hose, flowing off a car bonnet' – the stick never touched the metal surface itself. A piece of lobbed seashell also slowed and rolled off without touching the metal, as did a handful of fine sand.

'He felt slightly curious, 'peaceful', not at all fearful. After about ten minutes on watch, he may have 'nodded off' for a few minutes, for he sort of 'woke up with a bit of a start', and looked over the object. Nothing had changed, and after a few minutes more, he started to think about the dog. He got up and moved away inland from the disc to where the dog was, still somewhat agitated.

'He then walked back home with the dog, skirting well-around the disc area, arriving home a little before dark. He thought little more about the object, but *did not take the dog walking that way again – what could he have done; he couldn't have 'taken the thing home'?'*

'The house where he was staying alone had no telephone or newspaper delivery, and he had no television. He had no way of knowing at the time if anyone else had seen or reported the object – and didn't know who else would even be interested.'

There was, however, an article in the *'Christchurch Press'* on 4th February. Unbeknown to Cliff, many other nearby residents had witnessed the unusual craft.

One, a local electrician, had stopped his car, at about 8.45pm, when he thought there was a scrub fire in that area.

"I got out of my car to check the light. As I approached I heard an oscillating, whistling noise. I was astonished to see an object, about twenty feet wide, rise off the beach. It lifted to a height of about fifty feet. As it rose, the light gradually dimmed and I lost it from sight." When he later went to that part of the beach, he and a couple of friends found an area of flattened grass between two sand hills.

Other local witnesses reported seeing lights often travelling from north to south, in the sky, and more reports came from further away, including some Invercargill. Unfortunately, the meteorological radar at Christchurch was only operating between 4.15pm and 6pm, and had not detected anything.

1st May 1965

Terry Bell wrote in *'UFO Here?'*; *'While the sightings of laymen are usually debunked out of hand, there is a marked silence when 'trained' people come up with similar observations.*

'A classic example was in New Zealand on May 1st 1965. People in Wellington and Christchurch reported seeing a flight of strange objects in the sky, heading over the Tasman. They would certainly have been set to face the usual round of ridicule had not both the New Zealand and Australian air forces picked up seven UFOs over the Tasman at the same time. Civil Aviation also confirmed the sighting, and an aircraft crew, flying over the Tasman, also saw the flight.'

Wellington 31st May 1965

Between 4pm and 6pm, many witnesses reported seeing a large, grey, cylindrical craft over Mount Victoria. One sceptical journalist, in Broadcasting House, received a phone call, and when he and five newsroom colleagues, plus two office girls, went to the window, they could also see the strange object, which was shaped like an upside down umbrella. It was a cloudy day, but for about five minutes, they all watched the unusual object until it disappeared from view behind Mount Victoria.

The journalist, who later wrote up the incident for the local radio station and National TV, said that to him, the craft first appeared to be cigar-shaped, but then it changed, as if by a pulsating movement, and eventually reformed into a roundish ball, which sped off towards the western side of Wellington Harbour.

"Its acceleration was instantaneous. Its colour changed from luminous white to a dark grey, and was quite the most awe-inspiring sight I have ever seen in the sky!"

Many other residents also witnessed the same huge, grey, cylindrical craft. Several employees in the Air New Zealand offices watched for some time as an oval shaped object descended from the clouds, changed shape quite rapidly, and hovered over Mount Wellington. It moved with a slow 'tumbling' motion, which might have explained the perceived rapid change in shape. They thought it might have been about twenty feet in diameter.

Whilst the major radar installations in Wellington had not detected the object, there were no weather balloons up at the time.

Tasman Sea July 15th 1965

Mr. G. A. Morris was a mechanical engineer, on board the frigate HMNZS *'Otago'*, which had just left the Hauraki Gulf, and was on naval exercises, fifty miles into the Tasman Sea, heading along the west coast of the North Island.

At 1.15am, he suddenly spotted, in the clear, cloudless sky, a luminous, green, cigar-shaped object, heading in a NNW direction. Both ends were bright red, and he estimated it to be about 500ft in length, and flying at approximately 800mph, at an altitude of an estimated 6,000ft.

He was the only person on deck, and watched it for a minute or so, before it disappeared from view.

Rugged Island 13th November 1965

Two Invercargill fishermen, M. D. Hanning, skipper of the fishing boat *'Eleoneai'*, along with his friend Mr. W. Johnson, set off to tend to their cray pots, near Stewart Island. At 11.30am, they were about half a mile off Rugged Island when they saw a strange object rise about fifteen feet out of the sea.

'Spaceview' told of how the startled men described the 'craft' as being a tapered structure, about five feet high at the top, and twelve feet at the water line. About thirty feet away from it, there was another object – box shaped, about ten feet long and five feet high. The water was smooth, and the object in clear view, about 300 yards away. It had no markings, and was black or brown in colour. They could not detect any periscope or railing – nothing but the 'tower' and 'box' was visible.

The men watched for about twelve seconds, and felt some fear when there was a great surging of water, after which both objects had 'disappeared'. Both men felt rather frightened, and decided to head back to port. Over lunch, they discussed the incident, and rang Awarua Radio, to inquire if there were any submarines in the area.

Soon after, they received a message from the Navy, who interviewed them a couple of days later. Both men had seen a submarine before, and were certain that the objects they had witnessed were different, further, they had not mistaken them for whales or logs.

When the press suggested that the men had seen part of a Russian nuclear submarine, both the men and the Navy denied this. The Navy, through its spokesman, the Deputy Chief of Naval Staff, stated; " it was most unlikely that the object – whatever it might have been – was a submarine, because it would have been operating in an area where there were rocks, a definite submarine hazard. Besides, there was no logical reason for any submarine to be in that area."

Tauranga 1966

The *'Bay of Plenty Times'* reported on a frightening experience of a pig hunter, on his son Rod's farm.

One night, Maurice Brill, the pig hunter, was standing on the airstrip at "Tombstone Station', when he was 'buzzed' by an unidentified flying object. Rod, and colleague Jim Ewart were in a gully, beside the airstrip, trying to 'get a bead' on a pig which the dogs had bailed.

Maurice was getting a knife out of a vehicle parked on the airstrip, when he looked up to see the 'UFO' begin its sweep over the airstrip. The egg-shaped object looked to be the size of a car. It was humming as it passed overhead, at about fifty feet.

Jim also saw the object, and Maurice said; "It was too close for comfort. It gave me a fright, so I back pedalled!"

I wondered if extraterrestrials did not like us hunting and killing animals. This account brought to mind an incident which occurred sometime later, in Tasmania, Australia.

George and his family had lived on their property, fifty-five kilometres north of Hobart, for fifteen years without incident. Their farm consisted of rolling paddocks backed by sandstone hills with steep rocks and gullies. It had me wondering, animal mutilations aside, if some species of visitors do not like us killing our wildlife.

It all started in about July 1985, when George and his 16-year-old son Peter were shooting possums at the base of a hill on an adjoining property, about 2.5 kilometres away. Possums are a protected species in most parts of Australia, and George already had some carcasses, so Peter called to him to turn off the spotlight, (powered by a backpack battery), as he thought someone was coming.

George looked to see a bright blue object about five kilometres away in the sky. It came closer, and within a few minutes was only 200 metres away, not far above the ground. Some seven to eleven round blue lights were emitted from the top of the object, and they hung in a line about six to seven metres above it. It silently dropped vertically down and landed. It was surrounded by a bright blue glow which illuminated the whole area, including where George and Peter were standing.

The craft was about twenty to twenty-five metres tall and six to seven metres wide. It was bullet-shaped with a rounded top and a straight base. Halfway around the object was a ring, or ledge. After it touched down George felt something warm on his back - the twelve-volt battery in his backpack was starting to warm up and bubble. He grabbed the dead possums and told Peter they had to get back to the car one kilometre away. As they started to move the object began to make a noise. It was like a type of singing but unintelligible, like a foreign language.

They dropped the possums and left behind the rifle and battery (now cooled off) when they reached the car, and drove slowly home in the dark, without headlights. There was no sign of burning on George's skin, shirt or jumper, but the singlet underneath had a 15 centimetre burn hole.

South Canterbury 6th August 1966

It was only 4am on Saturday morning, and young David and Nicola got up earlier than intended as their father had erroneously set the chimes on the grandmother clock over two hours earlier than intended.

Thinking it was 6am, the children made some breakfast then went down to the pony paddock for an early morning ride. They noticed a fast moving yellow light coming from the west. It travelled to the north of where they were standing, followed a nearby creek and circled the town of Makikihi before coming back towards the youngsters' home.

It stopped and hovered about 5000 feet above a cattle stop, and slightly south-east of where David and Nicola were standing. The object was a glowing yellow; around the rim it had a row of coloured lights, and round the bottom of the dome it had more yellow lights. One row of lights would be on, and the other off, and they would alternate in this fashion. Underneath the craft were two larger yellow lights at each end.

The craft rocked gently up and down, and made a noise 'like a jet taking off', only much softer. David thought it was about ninety feet wide, as large as a two storey house, and looked like a 'car tyre with a hubcap on top'.

They watched for about five minutes, until Nicola became frightened. She returned to the house, and after a while, David followed. By the time their older brother got dressed and came out to have a look, the object had vanished.

About the same time, Mrs. M., who lived a few miles away, was driving east towards Makikihi when she saw a wingless craft, with lights along the side. At first it lit up the street behind her, but a few seconds later, crossed the road in front of her, and disappeared to the north.

About a year earlier, Mrs. Nossiter and her two children went down to the beach to collect shells. They saw a very bright, white light hovering over the breakers a short way up the beach to the north. It was about twelve feet wide, with a dome on top, and appeared to be rocking to and fro about ten feet above the water.

In her alarm, she unfortunately got her car bogged in the sand. She was frantic, and it took her and the two young boys nearly half an hour to free the vehicle. The strange craft was still there when they hastily left.

Taradale 1968

Fred Dickeson's *'Scientific Approach to Cosmic Understanding'* group in New Zealand published an interesting report in 1968.

Two Taradale youths had leapt out of their car, seconds before it crashed into a fruit shop window. Mr. Walker, one of the local residents, said that he ran outside as soon as he heard the crash, and saw the two boys who were hobbling from the scene, and trembling with fear.

It later transpired that after the lads had heard an explosion near the town dump, and seen a massive flashing object, rising from the ground, they reported the incident to local police, who laughed at them. After that, they set out on a regular 'UFO hunt', and the police laughed again when they made a second report.

Not to be deterred, they spotted another strange craft, and started following it around the town. Obviously, whatever intelligence that was operating the object, had enough of being trailed, and dive bombed the two youths in their car.

Mr. Walker, who employed one of the lads, said they told him that they were travelling at about thirty to forty mph, when one called out; "Bail out, it's got us...." and they both jumped. He told researchers the boys didn't want to talk about it anymore.

Napier Police, however, were more forthcoming, and had decided to accept the boys' excuse. They admitted that at least two constables had confirmed seeing strange lights in the sky, and many residents, who would no longer travel alone after dark, were jittery about flashing lights in the night sky, and ominous rumblings around the hills.

When Dow, the 19 year-old driver, who was none-the-less charged with dangerous driving in the Napier Magistrate's Court, Mr. Monaghan, who appeared on the lad's behalf, noted that as his passenger leapt from the vehicle, he kicked Dow's feet, causing him to lose control of the car.

After hearing considerable evidence of the youngsters' hunt for UFOs, the Magistrate, Mr. W. Dougall, declined Mr. Monaghan's offer to provide independent witnesses to the sightings of unusual objects in the sky, and dismissed the charge.

Kaingaroa North Island – end April 1968

Between 10.30pm and 11pm, Mr. and Mrs. McKenzie were returning home from Rotorua when they saw a light ahead, moving at about half treetop level. Fearing it may be an oncoming logging truck, they slowed down, but as they drew level with the turn-off, they realised it was a half-moon-shaped object, hovering three feet above the ground, close to the edge of the trees.

It was a goldy-orangey-yellow colour, and had three leg-like appendages hanging from underneath. It was about the size of an average car – ten to twelve feet across. Suddenly it took off vertically, silently and at high speed, raising dense clouds of dust.

Te Mata - Havelock North - 20th December 1968

At 11.20am, students at the Te Mata School, Havelock North, were quite frightened when they saw a strange craft hovering at close range, over an orchard near the school. Some of the children, who were near the pool, where the teacher was giving swimming lessons, yelled out; "Space Ship!", and drew everyone's attention to the object, which they estimated to be half the size of the pool.

It was touching the top of a poplar tree, about one hundred yards away from the playground, and making a 'clicking' noise, 'like a clock'. The craft was saucer-shaped, about twenty-five feet wide, with lights around the bottom, and a 'diamond-shaped' light on the dome. It was white on the bottom with a black band around the side, where there appeared to be a hatch.

One teacher said that suddenly the craft shot upwards, and travelled towards Hastings, leaving a vapour trail in its wake. Two other nearby residents also watched the strange craft, and Mrs. Berg said that it made a strange noise as it passed right over her house, before shooting upwards and going straight up into the sky. One teacher said he watched for about ten minutes as the object moved backwards and forwards over the town. It was too round to fit the description of any aircraft he knew, and the Bridge Pa aerodrome and Napier's Civil Aviation Department said that there were no aircraft in the area at 11.20am – the time of the sighting.

Palmerston North - Early January 1969

Early one morning, two men saw an extremely bright light coming down from the sky. It was a noiseless, cigar-shaped object, about thirty feet long, with a bright 'searchlight' at the front, and a slightly dimmer light at the rear. The witnesses, who were sure it was not an aeroplane, watched as it skimmed along over the paddocks. It hovered 300 feet above the ground for ten seconds, before moving away toward the Tararua Ranges.

Tauranga 12th May 1969

It was about 9.45pm when Allan Allingham and his wife Una were farewelling some guests at their home, when they all saw a strange craft, which flew swiftly towards them, before silently hovering about 350-500ft up, seventy yards away, before moving off in a westerly direction.

It was described as being a saucer-shape, like an inverted bowl, forty to fifty feet in diameter, with a rounded top turret, which was spinning during movement. Around the turret were three portholes emitting an intense bluish-white light.

Earlier in the day, at 2.40pm, Hilda Bliss, with a friend and three children, was travelling along the Te Puke-Mt. Maunganui highway. When they saw a bright, silvery object, which was hovering in the west-north-west sky, they slowed the car and watched for several minutes until it suddenly climbed vertically, at great speed, and vanished.

Elsthorpe – Hastings – 23rd June 1969

At 8.40 am, four youngsters, aged between nine and thirteen, who were walking down their driveways, off to catch the school bus, started to 'scream and run away', when a strange, multi-coloured flying object suddenly hovered about eight feet above the ground 200 yards away.

They said; "It first appeared behind a row of hills which are behind a farm over the road from us." It disappeared, and they saw it again in a paddock where one of their fathers was feeding cattle. When it was over the cattle, they started to run in all directions, possibly frightened by the strange, humming noise coming from the craft.

The unusual object, which had zoomed in like a streak of lightning, burst into a lot of colours, then shot away after a few seconds. It was not there by the time the school bus arrived, about ten minutes later, but when they arrived at Elsthorpe School, the teacher made them each draw what they had seen. Their sketches all depicted an object, as long as the school bus, but wider, with jagged edges, but varied in their impressions of shape from 'oval' to 'like a box'.

It is not known if it was relevant, but there was also a power failure in the area that morning.

Napier 25th June 1969

Only two days later, Napier businessman, Bernie Meredith, an estate agent and proprietor of a Napier dancehall, was going home at 2.30am, when he noticed that all the street lights were out. Suddenly he saw a typical 'flying saucer', hovering about a quarter of a mile away.

He stopped his car, and watched for three or four minutes. It was hovering about sixty feet above Marewa School, and was 'sheathed in an aluminium-like metal, with a row of lights beneath the rim, emitting a greeny-white phosphorescent glow'. Bernie decided to get a better look, and sped towards the object, with his car lights 'full on'.

As he came within one hundred yards of the 'disc', he could see it was much bigger than a bus; "..perhaps eighty feet across – and it was definitely a controlled craft. There was someone in it, alright, and once they spotted me, they were gone. It just went straight up into the clouds, and disappeared. Before this I had always treated flying saucers as hogwash, but what I saw was a real, solid object."

Ngatea 4th September 1969

This controversial case began in early September, when farmer Bert O'Neil found a sixty foot mysterious circle of a strangely affected patch of manuka on a run-off section of his fifty acre property, on the Hauraki Plains, about 25-30 miles N.N.W. of Waihi. A long line of twelve foot manuka, (or tea-tree) had died, and become quite 'white' looking compared to the surrounding green area. A large area of smaller scrub was also dead, and mysteriously charred bodies of dead spiders were also found.

As soon as the media learned of the discovery, flocks of sightseers had invaded the property, and trampled the area, disturbing and destroying what may have been valuable evidence. Many had souvenired samples of the manuka scrub, making later investigations even more difficult. There were some ground traces, indentations and marks or holes, however it was not known if they had been caused by the countless number of visitors swarming over the site.

It was a month before the experts were called in, however none of their findings ever confirmed that UFOs were responsible for this 'circle' or any others reported about the same time.

Official findings varied somewhat. The physics department of the University of Otago could find no trace of radiation, however a 'leading horticulturist', Mr. Stuart-Menzies, claimed that it was radio-active, and the vegetation had been 'cooked from the inside out', by some form of short-wave, high frequency radiation. He concluded that; *'Some outside object appears to have landed on the spot, and on taking off, emitted the energy which cooked the plants'.*

The Department of Scientific and Industrial Research did due diligence in their research, and October 1969, Mr. Talboys, the Minister of Science, announced that the manuka had been killed by a fungus known as Saprophytic fungus, which was living in the dead tissue. His statement was accompanied by a substantial detailed report of the analysis conducted by his scientists.

The Auckland University UFO Research Group, were disappointed with the DSIR findings, as their University's Botany Department had confirmed that saprophytes only attack dead plants. They can only follow death, not cause it! This had been confirmed by other experts from all over the country. Based on further professional advice, they also concluded that the manuka had probably been killed long before it had been discovered – most probably by 245-T weedkiller, which was possibly dropped from an aircraft at the time of a south-westerly wind. Other experts, including L. Matthews , a scientist from the Hamilton Raukura Soil Research Station, also considered that the damage to the manuka had been caused by the spraying of a weedkiller, possibly from the air.

Not everybody was convinced. Investigator, Harvey Cooke, who visited the site, believed that the markings were made by a 'heavy object making a soft landing'. He also mentioned a report received, not long before the Ngatea discovery, from Paeroa, of a pulsating light travelling in a direct line to where the circle was discovered.

Scientific analysis was further hampered when a couple of self-professed 'psychics' also entered the debate, claiming contact with the aliens who had landed on the spot.

However, there were other similar cases investigated. About a year previously, two strange circular marks were found in the grass, in two different paddocks, on a farm in Honeymoon Valley in the Mangamuka Hills. The Department of Scientific and Industrial Research analysed them as being an obscure and unknown fungus.

In late 1969, two mysterious circular patches of burnt grass were found on the side of a steep hill on a farm near Rotorua. One circle, 53 feet in diameter, was very distinct, and the smaller one, 30 feet in diameter, had almost faded away.

The property owner, Mr. C. Johnson, said that when they approached the area, his horse reared up, and refused to go any nearer. Mr. D. Ridsworth, a geologist from DSIR in Rotorua, could offer no explanation, and sent samples to the Department of Scientific and Industrial Research for further analysis.

Puketutu 8th October 1969

On Wednesday, 8th October 1969, Mr. Charles Blackmore noticed a flattened, perfect circle of water weeds, about fourteen feet across, which had appeared overnight on a 'dew pond' up on the steep hills behind his farmhouse. There was a sickly-sweet smell in the air, and his horse and dog, as well as the cows in the paddock, refused to drink from, or go near the pond, however cattle in a nearby field seemed unaffected. Four wild ducks, which had lived there for some time, had disappeared, as had an unusually large frog population.

Mr. Blackmore suffered a headache, which lasted three weeks, and the cows became lethargic, developed a nasal discharge, and black spots on one side of their bodies. The herd's usual milk production fell by fifty percent, and the vet was at a loss to explain it.

Samples from the pond indicated no atomic radiation, however it was discovered that intense electromagnetic radiation had destroyed the vegetation, which died off, turned brown and began to sink.

On 14th January 1970, at 4.30am, when Mr. Blackmore was taking his cows for milking, they suddenly 'went silly' – running around the paddock, and sniffing in the direction of the pond. They refused to go into the 'cow-bales' or let their milk down once inside. The 'dry-stock' were also affected; black cattle huddled in a corner, the dogs were crouched and quiet, and turkeys hunched in their nearby pen.

On a neighbour's farm, other cows went berserk, running around, sniffing the air, and also looking towards Mr. Blackmore's pond. Mrs. Blackmore, hearing the sound of bulls bellowing and dogs barking, commented on the pandemonium, and that there was a strange pungent smell in the air.

After milking, Mr. Blackmore went to the pond to check, and beside the strong odour, there was another identical circle of swirled, dead reeds, which hadn't been there the previous day. The pond, itself, was brown and muddy, as it it had been swirled up. His headaches returned, as did the reduced milk production. The results of many tests on the pond and soil were inconclusive.

Mr. Blackmore also advised investigators that about a month later, he had sighted a metallic saucer, twenty feet in diameter, and nine feet high, with a stationary one foot central strip. Both top and bottom sections were rotating in a clockwise direction. On another occasion, during the night, an object was seen hovering over the cowshed. It shot out a beam of light in Mr. Blackmore's direction, and he immediately felt as if a band were being tightened around his head. Another time an object had been seen hovering over the pond, and other members of his family also had sightings.

On September 14th 1970, at the same time the newspapers were reporting UFO sightings in the area, another circle of swirled reeds had appeared in the pond overnight. Was the damage to his pond and cows due to a UFO? We may never know. Due to many authorities considering the earlier Ngatea event being a 'false alarm', plus several obscure reports of 'circles' in the local fields and paddocks, they had backed away from investigating this subsequent incident.

Circles and Lichen

In 1971, following all the reports of strange 'circles', especially some at Taupo and Wanaka, Bryan Dickeson wrote a lengthy article about the incidence of lichen, which was often the cause of some, but not necessarily all, of the reports being received from excited property owners.

He also considered this explanation could possibly apply to other recent reports received from Queenstown, however it did not account for four 'circular bands', noticed by some mountain climbers at the foothills of 'The Remarkables'. One circle had a 2'6" band, forming the outer part of a 25ft diameter circle, another was double the size.

Tauranga December 1969

During the Christmas holidays, a Police Sergeant and seven other on duty policemen were returning to Tauranga at about 1am, when they saw a strange light over the aerodrome. At first they thought it was an aircraft, but soon realised it was something else. As it moved towards the hills, it resembled a 'bus' moving through the sky. It moved around and below the 761ft mountain, and then hovered over the harbour entrance. They watched as it travelled about two miles out over the sea, before suddenly shooting up and away at an angle.

CHAPTER FIVE

PILOTS, the MILITARY & GROUND INSTALLATIONS

There have been several instances in the past when unidentified craft have been sighted by flight crews in New Zealand, and tracked on radar. Pilots are perhaps the most expert and reliable of all witnesses, and it is hard to dispute the radar evidence:

Both *'CSINZ'* and the *'Australian Flying Saucer Magazine'* reported that on May 24th 1954, pilots Wasser, Hodder and Ferrier, were in a Cessna, at an altitude of 3,000ft, flying east from New Plymouth airport. At about 7am, as they were nearing Tahora, all saw three giant oval discs hovering about 7,000ft above them. They were reddish/orange in colour, and were emitting a reddish colour flame. The pilots said that when they flew on in the same direction, after about three minutes, a number of others appeared, apparently flying in single line formation. Suddenly they all climbed steeply, and disappeared at great speed.

Even in the 1950s, N.Z. authorities were trying to explain away reports made by the most competent witnesses of all – pilots and experienced airmen.

Harold Fulton, president of *CSI*, documented the following incident, which occurred on 31st October, 1955.

Captain Rainbow made the following official report to the Director of Air Intelligence in Wellington;

'On the night of 31st October, 1955, I was Captain of Flight 108 proceeding from Wellington to Auckland. We departed from Paraparaumu in excellent weather, and conditions remained so until we ran into a warm front which was lying across out track at Raglan Reporting Point, and extended out to the west where it lay in a N.E.-S.W. direction.

'At sunset, visibility was excellent, due to a full moon and little cloud over the air route. At 2006 hours, as I was looking towards the southwest direction, a very brilliant light caught the corner of my eye. This light was positioned above 3/8ths cloud, the top of which appeared to be about 600ft, and also below scattered middle cloud.

'My first impression was that it was a meteor, or a planet sitting in the Southern declination, but after closer investigation, I could see that it was moving say about 2,000ft above the cloud tops, and it was changing light intensity from a bright, hard light to a brilliant light in a cycle of approximately 3 seconds and changing colour from white-yellow-orange to red.

'It appeared to be to the west of Waitara and at the same altitude as us. I then asked the co-pilot, F/O S. Trounce, to have a look towards our tail, and to tell me what he thought the light could be. At first his impressions were the same as mine, but he could not understand the change of brilliance in the light, its colour, or the fact that it was overtaking us at the same altitude. He also suggested that I open the window to eliminate any refraction error, but it made no difference to the object.

'I then asked him to go to the cabin and ask a Mr. Tuckett, who is a Civilian Aviation Officer, and an experienced pilot, to watch the light and to ask if he thought it was a planet. During the co-pilot's absence, I called Wellington Control and asked if there were any known aircraft to the west of New Plymouth, and their answer was negative. I next called them and told them there was a bright light to the west of New Plymouth, and to ask Flight 135 if he could see it: the last part of my message was jammed by Wellington Control, who at that time were doing just that. I next called up and said that this bright light was changing colour, and passing to the West of us, at a distance of, if I remember rightly, 10-15 miles, and at the same time, giving them incorrect call sign of Flight 135.

'F/O Trounce then returned to the cockpit, when at this time the object was just west of our wingtip and still at the same altitude as ourselves. Our Autopilot was engaged on the same course of 330 degrees compass as it had been for the last 10 minutes before Chura check point, and this I checked to ensure that I was not turning towards the west, and so could explain the object's changed position in relation to our course. I could also see the object flying in and out of a few tops of the cloud, which was building up as we approached the front.

'After a further close look and discussion with the co-pilot, I then told him to go back to the cabin and waken Air Commodore Cohen and get him to have a look at this object and so confirm what we were seeing. As the co-pilot was in the cabin, we entered the front, and knowing that there was no aircraft on the air route, I climbed to 9,000ft, whereupon the object was easily picked up below us *and ahead. After several more minutes observation, I obtained our clearance to come down to 4,000ft in preparation for landing at Auckland, and so lost contact upon entering cloud again.*

'During the descent the co-pilot returned to the cockpit and informed me that the Air Commodore stated that it was a planet, and took no further interest and went back to sleep. Then I went back to the cabin and spoke to Mr. Tuckett, and asked if he thought this was a planet, and to this he said no, and that he had never seen anything like that before. He also noticed the object overtaking us and changing its position in relation to us. A Mr. Hume, in the seat ahead of him, also confirmed all that Mr. Tuckett, Trounce and myself had seen. I then approached the Air Commodore and asked his opinion, to which he remarked that it was a planet, low down on the horizon, but he made no further comment when I said that it had definitely passed us at 8,000ft.

Upon arrival at Whenuapai, I notified the officer on duty at Whenuapai, and as far as I was concerned, there the matter rested.'

Harold Fulton investigated the incident thoroughly, and later wrote; *'I regret to report that the official investigation of this incident has apparently climaxed just the way we expected, and even predicted on stage at our public meeting. The N.A,C. crew were called to Wellington and interviewed by the Director of Air Intelligence. At the close of a day-long study of the incident, and a thorough checking of the Planet Venus's position in the western sky, and its setting time, the playing back of the tape recorded radio conversations between Air Control and the crew during the observation, and eliminating the possibility of other aircraft being in the area, Intelligence Officers could not identify the source or find a natural phenomena explanation of the 'Flying Light'*

'A press statement was released and published on November 5th. Close on this announcement, the press reported on November 8th; 'that on new reckonings and fixings of the Planet Venus's position and setting time, provided to the investigators by Mr. I. L. Thomson, Director of Carter Observatory, Wellington, Mr Halstead stated that the Air Force Investigators now agreed that the Planet Venus could have been the cause of the 'Flying Light' observation, however the speed and movement of the light reported by Captain Rainbow remained unexplained. Mr. Halstead, Deputy Minister of Defence, concluded by stating "that all other press releases made during this investigation were not from official sources."

..... 'This statement constitutes a rather nasty rebuke to the Air Force Intelligence people, who were responsible for the investigation and released to the press their day-to-day progress, and objective search for the truthful answer to the mystery.'

Auckland 10th June 1956

Leading Airman Brian Lovestock was walking his dog at about 9.30pm. It was a cold, wet night, and the wind was blowing strongly from the northeast, when he noticed something bright, moving slowly against the wind.

He told *'CSINZ'*; "I immediately looked up, and to my great shock and fear, I saw above and behind the houses on my half-right, about forty degrees angle, and 200 feet from the ground, an object which had these characteristics; - The object appeared to be hovering, and moving slowly eastward, it was like an upside-down saucer with bell-shaped top.

"The 'saucer' glowed, or should I say emanated a blue-white light. It also grew dim and bright alternatively, as if it were a light fixed on a dimmer, with a slide moved up and down. The light did not seem to be reflected to any great extent, as would the lights of a car.

"I'm afraid I was so shocked and scared, I did not notice any mechanical protuberances or windows. During this whole business, I had a most uncanny feeling as if someone or something was 'sizing me up'. This passed when the object suddenly took off at a terrific speed straight up. After it had disappeared, I raced for the nearest street light, and stood under it. It took me some time to 'cool down' and sort things out."

7th August 1956

The following year, *'The Taumarunui Press'* covered the following account. At 4.10pm, experienced Hamilton pilot, J. Ferri, was driving a few miles south of Te Kuiti when he saw a glint of something shining in the sun. He said; "I glanced idly up at it, and away again, then experienced a 'double take' as I realised its shape was not that of an aircraft. The object could be described as a disc or sphere, but whichever it was to my vision, it was perfectly round and shining with steady brilliance, it was clear-cut against the blue sky.

"While watching the road, I glanced back several times. Its motion, upwards and southward ahead of me, was effortless, but from the rate at which its size diminished, its speed must have been fantastic. Its height, when I first noticed it, was much greater than it had seemed as an aircraft, and I had it in perfect view for twelve to fifteen seconds before it grew too small and faint and a small cloud finally lost it to view."

Panmure 3rd September 1956

The next month, R. McKechnie, made the following report to '*CSINZ';* 'I saw an object, in the northern sky, from my residence at about 1845 hours on the 3rd September 1956. The fuselage appeared to me to be cylindrical, and the proportion of length to depth was approximately 7:1. From my home, it appeared slightly less than the thickness of an ordinary pencil held at arm's length. It was climbing towards the west at an angle of approximately 25-30 degrees....It's height and speed were difficult to estimate, but I considered it to be over the North Shore at a height of probably 7,000ft and its speed something in excess of 300 knots. There was a slightly blue-tinged light at the nose, and an impressive exhaust trail.

'I was a pilot during the war, and have seen a sufficient number of aircraft, both day and night, to be convinced that the object I saw was definitely not what we regard as an orthodox aircraft, and neither was it, as has been suggested by some who did not see it, a meteor. The outlines of the fuselage were clearly defined, particularly the after end.'

Although it is not known if the craft was of earthly or extraterrestrial origin, his report was substantiated by many other witnesses.

At the same time, in Auckland, four members of the Girven family saw 'a long, cigar-shaped, brilliant white light moving rapidly across the sky from east to west.' Mrs. Girven and her two daughters, thought it was a 'propelled' object, but her husband, who, during the war, had served four-and-a-half years in the Air Force, said it was not one of our planes, as had been suggested in the local papers.

Numerous witnesses, including Mr Farnsworth and his son who were walking their dog along an Auckland road, also saw the same object. Mr. Spence of Whangarei said it was travelling faster than any known aircraft, and multiple witnesses from the suburb of Wellsford, where the craft passed directly overhead, claimed it was definitely 'spinning'.

Waiuku 7th November 1957

It was a clear night, with a brilliant near-full moon when, at 10.45pm., R. Pollard, an ex-RNZAF Flight Engineer, No. 5FB Squadron, was returning to his home in Waiuku. Upon rounding a bend in the main road, he was confronted by an unusual object hovering over the next bend, half a mile up ahead. It was a brilliantly illuminated, flattened sphere, about fifty feet above the road. He likened it to an 'electric light bulb', with an antenna protruding upwards, in a narrow pyramid form, and glowing green in colour.

He stopped his car, and just before he got out to get a better look, the strange craft, as if aware of his presence, quickly ascended a few hundred feet higher, before moving slowly away. Then suddenly, it dived down to the edge of Lake Pokuroa at a very low altitude. It then rose again, and hovered above a trig. station on a sand hill.

He raced home, and then he and his wife drove back up to a good vantage point. They both watched the object, still hovering over the sand hill. It soon moved off southwards, following the sand hills along the coast, at a speed of about forty knots. Altogether, it had been in view for about fifteen minutes.

Woodbourne 1962

We must still ask the question as to whether these strange unidentified objects that were being seen in New Zealand skies were in fact extraterrestrial visitors or earthly prototypes of our own?

On 13th April 1962, the *'New Zealand Herald'* published a news item for which they had received little explanation; *'A C124 Globemaster, of the United States Air Force, landed at the Woodbourne RNZAF station, Blenheim, yesterday afternoon. It unloaded an object, thirty-six feet long, which resembled the articulated section of a furniture removal van – its long aluminium body was windowless, and gave no hint as to what it contained. Neither did the American crew – "It is just a box we loaded back home for delivery here. As it says on it, from the University of Denver to the RNZAF base, Woodbourne, Project Longbank."*

'No further details were available at Woodbourne, but on January 29th, the Prime Minister, Mr. Hollyoake, said that Blenheim would become the site of a joint American-New Zealand aero-space research centre, which would study aero-space disturbances and their effect on radio communications.'

In 1967, the Dickeson's *'Scientific Approach to Cosmic Understanding'* Newsletter contained the interesting, following report;

'Eccentrics on Holiday'.

'The first indication that anything was afoot at Woodbourne came in February 1962, when four Americans in civilian dress flew in from the University of Denver, Colorado and began radio research at the time. (Colorado University had been awarded the Grant of $300,000 for research into the 'Space Brothers' and Saucers.) The men had camped in tents on the airfield and RNZAF personnel were told not to inquire what they were doing. If they found out, they were not to tell anyone. A station notice told the New Zealanders that anyone asking what the four men were doing was to be told that they were eccentric Americans on holiday.

'After a time the men returned to the United States, and in April electronic equipment began to arrive at the Base from the United States. On May 15th, 1963 – several months before the general election – Mr. Holyoake announced that an agreement had been reached between the two countries for a joint aerospace communications research centre at Woodbourne.

'A fortnight later, a group of about ten USAF technicians arrived in Auckland as the advance party to get the project started. A 'Herald' reporter who met them at Whenuapai airport was told that the scientific studies at Woodbourne would be a long-term project. The head of the advance group, Capt. M. J. Closs, said that those with families would remain in New Zealand for three and four year terms.

'Capt. Closs, who headed the project until he returned home, several months ago, confirmed at the time that as the unit began work, additional technicians and equipment would arrive. The subsequent build-up has been such that the Americans have caused a minor economic boom in the small farming town. One of the things that has caused much puzzlement that the Americans import their cars, furniture, stoves, refrigerators and most home appliances from the United States, instead of patronising local firms. It is thought that this custom was due to initial misjudgement in logistics by Washington planners than to a desire by the Americans to be different.

'Since the start of the mini-invasion by the Americans, specific details about the studies themselves have never been released and even most RNZAF personnel

at Woodbourne, were known to be curious but ignorant of the goings-on in the large hanger used by the Americans until recently. Security was such that only several members of the RNZAF staff were allowed to enter the building.

'The 'Herald' science correspondent, who visited the Base in 1963, was told only in general terms by Capt. Closs that the Americans were doing aerospace radio research. He was refused entry to the hanger. The hangar, which is known to have an aerial system built into its roof, was the sole centre for operations for 'Project Longbank', (its official code name), until early 1966. At this time, the Americans leased a large area of land on the farming plains at Riverlands, about four miles east of Blenheim.

'There, without fanfare or a line of publicity, they erected a complex aerial system of large steel towers and leaning aluminium poles. It stretched for about half a mile. The aerial system, within a mile of the southern motorway, could be seen by forewarned motorists and came as a surprise to many Blenheim residents, who had been accustomed only to covert activity from noncommittal airmen. Close to the aerial system was a mobile caravan, which housed control electronic equipment. It was constantly manned by technicians working in shifts through the day and night.

'The surprise local residents received when the system was erected, was more than matched when the vast installation was quietly dismantled nearly a year later and the Westinghouse equipment carted back to the Base. When it was standing, the only security measures evident were a 'trespassers prohibited' sign on the road leading to the aerial site and a deep natural moat encircling it. It is known that a member of the local aero club had the number of his plane noted by watching Americans when he circled over the system out of curiosity.

'These facts are known about the project; - The Americans are in direct radio contact with an unknown Government agency in Washington, to whom they are always relaying data. This is known often to take up many hours at a stretch. Commenting on this, Deputy Prime Minister, Mr. Marshall, said; "I have not inquired as to the frequency with which the unit communicates with Washington; but it is the information which it collects that is analysed and collated there. It would be natural for any communication to be regular and frequent."

'No New Zealanders are believed to be working directly with the Americans, in spite of the fact that the project was announced as a joint one. Regarding this,

Mr. Marshall said that; "..the agreement does not provide for the joint manning of the facilities as appropriate although, as far as I am aware, no need for this has so far been seen."

'The New Zealand scientific establishment is not known to have received information from the Americans in spite of a statement by Mr. Holyoake in 1965 that the then program was of 'considerable benefit to New Zealand'. Mr. Marshall said; "data from the project has been made available to us."

'The American equipment is attended to 24 hours a day, every day of the week, and many of the off-duty men are kept 'on-call' for emergencies of some sort. They must remain close to a telephone. The Americans sometimes receive fleeting visits from high ranking USAF officers, and are believed to have had a scrambled teleprinter link with Wellington.

'These facts, fitted into an all-encompassing mosaic, reveal a picture of activity at Blenheim that has left many residents fascinated. They point, as a cause for concern, to the recent move by the Americans to a new operations centre at the end of the aerodrome. There, hundreds of yards from anyone, the men now work in conspicuous isolation, in their brilliantly lit, air-conditioned building, which has only one window.'

N.Z. researcher Tony Brunt said the agreement between America and New Zealand closely paralleled their 'Deep Freeze' agreement made on Antarctic operations. He also made the following comments; 'More than forty American technicians – most of them with families – live in and around Blenheim, and daily travel to their tightly guarded headquarters at Woodbourne, several miles from the farming township. For many Blenheim folk the nature of the American's work does not appear as clear-cut or innocent as the government has indicated – simply because of the apparent secrecy in which it is shrouded.

'Although many of the airmen have married Blenheim girls, and mix freely in the community, they never discuss their work with outsiders. Whenever conversation starts to head in that direction, they always change the subject. "And", as said one resident recently; "if you ask them point blank what they are doing, they start to stammer." This stammering, whether real or imagined, has sparked many theories on what the Americans are supposedly up to."

Given the original 'Grant' made to the Colorado University, one wonders at the real purpose of this secretive activity. Was it in any way connected to the UFO sightings over New Zealand, or perhaps the rumours of an alien base further south in the Antarctica?

26th March 1963

RNZAF Flying Officer Hosie who was piloting a Canberra light bomber, forty miles northeast of Ahakea RNZAF Base, sighted an unidentified object flying above his altitude of nearly 20,000ft, and apparently beyond the radar range of ground installations at Wellington.

Hosie had spotted a rapidly flashing, bright white light ahead of him, and it was travelling in an easterly direction at approximately 390 knots, the same speed as the Canberra. For a full minute two flashes per second were observed. Although there were no other known aircraft in the area, Hosie could not investigate further as he was required to complete his flight exercise.

12th January 1965

In 1999, the Australian '*Ufologist*' magazine published the following account; '*Thirty-four years ago, on 12th January 1965, a DC-3 transport plane took off from Whenuapai, New Zealand, for a flight to Kaipara. As the twin-engine propeller plane flew over Kaipara Harbour, a broad estuary sixty miles north-west of Auckland, the pilot, Capt. Kirkpatrick, spotted an unusual gleam in the water below – an unidentified submerged object or USO.*

'*He was about one-third of the way across Kaipara Harbour, when he saw what he at first believed to be a stranded gray-white whale in an estuary. As he veered his DC-3 for a closer look at the object, it became evident to him that he was observing a metallic structure of some sort.*'

Capt. Kirkpatrick noted; "....that the thing was perfectly streamlined and symmetrical in shape....had no external surfaces or protrusions....appeared metallic with the suggestion of a hatch on top....was resting on the bottom of the estuary and headed towards the south as suggested by the streamlined shape...was harboured in no more than thirty feet of water....was not shaped like a normal submarine but approximately one hundred feet in length with a diameter of fifteen feet at its widest part."

'*After he filed his flight report, the Royal New Zealand Navy told Capt. Kirkpatrick .... 'that it would have been impossible for any known model of submarine to have been in that particular area due to the configuration of harbour and coastline.'*

In fact, *'NZSSRG'*, North Island, advised that 'Kirkpatrick' was actually a pseudonym used by Capt. Bruce Cathie, who later became very involved in research, and wrote several books.

13th January 1965

The next day, at 8.40pm, Capt. Shannon and his Qantas Electra aircrew, headed to Sydney, and 300 miles west of Auckland, tracked seven mysterious objects on their radar. The strange craft, which were flying eastward in a 'V' formation at 45,000ft., were also confirmed by the radar at New Zealand's Civil Aviation Department.

Later that night, lighted objects were seen over Lower Hutt and Grey Lynne, and just after midnight by a man fishing near Rangitoto.

Apparently the RNZAF preferred to write the objects off as 'ice crystals' whilst the RAAF theorised them to be 'high flying military aircraft'. There were no commercial flights in the area, and neither Air Forces had planes in the sky at the time. The *'Flying Saucer Review'* who published an account of the incident, noted; *'It was later reported in Sydney that unidentified aircraft had been plotted, flying at high altitudes, over the Tasman Sea. Urgent, top-secret investigations were being carried out by the RAAF and RNZAF to try to establish the identity of the formation......they were believed to be service aircraft capable of high speeds and long-range performance.'*

When reviewing the authorities' finding of a 'natural cause' for the incident, one researcher wrote; *'Well, here we have two possibilities, one 'birds' and the other, 'ice crystals'. But don't you think it is stretching the imagination a bit too far to endeavour to pretend, that with all the wonderful things being discovered, we now have supersonic birds which are jet propelled, and ice crystals flying over the Tasman Sea, splitting up and leaving seven vapour trails?'*

Auckland International Airport - 3rd December 1967

In his book *'Harmonic 695'*, Bruce Cathie wrote of how airport employees often see strange objects in the sky, or unidentified returns on their radar screens, but do not speak out for fear of losing their jobs.

Two of them confided in Bruce about an incident on 3rd December 1967: One said; *"While working at the airport, I saw two silvery-to-pale-lemon lights cross the sky from SSW to NNE. They were convex on both sides, and on the upper side was a small dome. They flew together for a short time until the lower one began to make sharp alterations in its altitude, zig-zagging up and down....They finally disappeared from sight in a bank of cloud to the north.'*

The second witness confirmed these details, but added that they were both travelling at an exceptional speed, in excess of a thousand miles per hour.

1968

RNZAF Orion Aircraft were conducting a routine exercise off the coast of the North Island one cloudy afternoon, when radar control reported a UFO travelling at forty knots, from north to south, about thirty miles off the coast. The Orion was requested to check, and approached on an intercepting course. The Orion's radar locked onto the object, but the crew could see nothing. The invisible object then lost altitude and a whirlpool like eddy was visible on the surface of the sea.

Again that year, radar returns were inconclusive. The co-pilot and crew of a Viscount airliner, flying north to Auckland from Wellington, at 19,000ft, were advised by radar operators at Auckland Airport that three stationary objects, spaced at regular intervals, had appeared on their screen. The crew could not see the objects, which suddenly disappeared off the screen.

1968 Tauranga

In 1968 the *'Auckland Star'* reported that *'An unidentified object was tracked by Department of Civil Aviation radar observers in Auckland from Waihi almost as far south as Tauranga. The UFO was then seen by two Tauranga Aero Club members south-east of Tauranga Airport. They observed 'a long, white cigar-shaped object' for a few minutes before it disappeared in the south-east. They immediately reported the sighting to Tauranga Airport.'*

There were no known aircraft in the area, and radar had tracked the strange object travelling between eighty to one hundred knots between Waihi to Tauranga.

On July 29th, the *'Auckland Star'* made further mention of the subject; *'Unidentified flying objects continue to be sighted in New Zealand skies, according to Captain B.C. Cathie, of Auckland, a National Airways Corporation pilot.*

'In recent weeks an object had been picked up on radar at Auckland International Airport, said Capt. Cathie. A RANZAF Orion, working from the airport was notified and used its radar to track the object, which slowed to a speed of only 45 miles an hour.

'Capt. Cathie and his co-pilot recently spotted a UFO on the west coast of the North Island, and there was another report, he said, of three such objects seen flying together.'

29th November 1968

The *'Evening Star'* newspaper reported on three unidentified objects which were sighted by two Wanganui men in the early hours of the morning as they flying from Wanganui to Fordell. The pilot, A. Harding, and his passenger, R. Peddie, first saw the lights, which were separate, and initially thought they were the navigational lights of a plane heading towards them. They radioed the Ohakee Air Force Base, who said that they had no aircraft out on low-flying night exercises.

Peddie wanted Harding to fly closer, for a better look, but suddenly the three lights, which had been in a triangular formation, split-up. One disappeared behind a ridge, another seemed to land or hover very close to the ground, and the third stayed directly above it. Although their shape was not easy to define, they seemed to be relatively large. After two or three minutes, they re-grouped and disappeared.

Mr. Peddie said; "We tried to find a logical explanation, but could not. I was not a believer in unidentified objects before, but I am now!"

Cook Strait, 4th September 1969

The pilot, Captain Cullum, and co-pilot, First Officer Faircloth, of a Straits Air-Freight Express were above Cook Strait and saw a flashing, bright blue light travelling about two miles away, and below them, at 3,000 feet with an estimated speed of 25 knots. Capt. Cullum was an experienced aviator who obtained his 'wings', during WW2, in both Canada and the RNZAF. For some years after, he flew as a Captain with British Airways before returning to New Zealand.

They watched it for over two minutes, and countered sceptics by stating that the only known object capable of staying aloft at that speed was a helicopter, "and choppers don't give off a blue light." Their credibility was supported by Wellington Radar station who confirmed tracking a blue pulsating light over the Cook Strait.

Some ninety minutes later Faircloth was making a return flight to Wellington, when he spotted the mystery objet again. This time it appeared as a cluster of lights, some fifteen miles distant, off the coast of the South Island, in the vicinity of Cape Campbell beacon. Radar confirmed it was the same object they had initially reported, and they were still tracking it.

Hawkes Bay area
Due to some confusion in the date of this next incident, my colleague Bryan Dickeson kindly provided me with the original report produced by Wynn Craven, who interviewed the witness twelve days after the event:

Waipukurau Aerodrome, 30th October 1969
Mr. J. Cudby, of Central Hawkes Bay Security Services, was making his regular security patrol at 3.10 a.m. with his six-year-old Alsatian dog. The first thing he noticed was that the flock of young sheep, which grazed on the Aero Club's ground, were all bunched up in one corner, as if something had frightened them. He parked his station wagon, switched off the headlights, and let the dog out for a run.

As he walked to the clubhouse door he heard a noise, which he initially assumed came from a train on the nearby railway track. As he tried the lock, he noticed three "out of place" lights reflected high in the glass door panel. These were different from the reflections of the lights from the town, a mile away. He could hear his dog growling from the station wagon, and when he looked back, he was amazed to see the three lights, two green and one red, in the sky, just above and to the right of his vehicle. The lights were alternating – white, green, red, green, and beaming down to the ground, illuminating a fifty-foot area below. They were at about telephone pole-height and he could see that they were actually attached to the turret portion of a big, saucer-shaped object.

The dog was now whimpering, racing round and round the station wagon. Cudby, who admitted to being frightened, hurried back to the vehicle and brought his centre mounted spotlight to bear on the object, about 300 feet away. He could see the object, about sixty feet long and twelve feet high, with a perfectly smooth surface like stainless steel. There appeared to be no joints, rivets or hatches in the metallic surface. It was moving sideways, to-and-fro, over a seven to eight foot span, and it was still emitting a constant, loud pitched, humming noise.

Mr.Cudby then reported that, after circling it three times; "As if alerted by the spotlight, several things happened. The light beams underneath suddenly brightened to the same intensity as the turret lights. Within about one second the to-and-fro motion stopped, and the noise built up to a high pitch. The whole craft tilted down at the right hand side, and it made off at high speed, its leading edge slightly down, and climbing at about a fifteen degree angle to the southwest.

"The dog was still madly racing around the car, and I walked to the corner of the hanger, where a windsock was rotating wildly before it returned to its normal limp position for the windless night. I walked across the wet grass and noticed that the area underneath where the object was hovering was very warm and dry."

Investigator, Wynn Craven, who interviewed Mr. Cudby, found him to be a decent, clean living, non-drinking family man. He finalised his report by saying, *'The witness now returned to his vehicle and caught his dog between his knees, as it was still circling the station wagon. Putting the dog inside he drove off feeling really frightened....He quickly went to the railway station. as is his custom, to have a cup of tea with the porter on duty. By this time the dog had quietened down, but the porter remarked to him that he looked as though he had just seen a ghost, and asked what had happened. Cudby related his story to the porter.*

'His patrol now over, he returned to his home at 4am, and awoke his wife and related to her what he had seen before retiring to bed. At 10am he went to the police station, to report what he had seen, but was ridiculed by the person in charge, Sgt. Scannell. He then went to the Waipukurau office of the 'Napier Daily Telegraph' and the story was published in the issue of the same day.'

While some were sceptical, a Mr. Grant was travelling through Hawkes Bay to Gisborne at about the same time when he saw a circular object about 100 feet above the ground. It had gradually gained height and abruptly took off to the south. Three other residents, who lived close to the airport, reported hearing the noise, and that their sheep were very disturbed.

The next day, 1st November 1969, the Napier *'Daily Telegraph'* published a report from Bob Strahl who was awakened in the early hours of the morning by a 'fantastic noise'. He looked out of his window to see a 'flying saucer' hovering near the Marine Parade.

It was like a large fluorescent light, and he said it was saucer-shaped, about twenty feet wide, and hovering approximately fifty feet over the stretch of green near the Hastings Street railway crossing. After a few seconds it suddenly 'whisked away at tremendous speed' towards the sea.

Christchurch 1970

In 1970 the Christchurch radar station was tracking a meteorological balloon when they encountered a second unexpected signal coming from an object way beyond the capabilities of any known craft. It was climbing at a rate of 7,000 feet per minute, its speed increasing with altitude. The radar station could no longer continue tracking it when it reached over 63,000 feet.

November 1971

Christchurch meteorological radar tracked another repeat phenomenon which defied explanation. The radar station was also tracking a meteorological balloon, about seventy miles away, and at a height of about 30,000ft, when it picked up a stronger signal and latched onto it. The object on the screen was also moving at the incredible rate of 7,000ft a minute, increasing its speed as it got higher. At 61,274 ft., the velocity of the object became so great, the radar station could no longer hold it.

F.W. Borthwick, from Met. Radar Christchurch, commented that at the moment of acquiring this target, it appeared as though the craft had seen our constant level balloon, and had turned off its predominately northwest heading to examine the balloon; "An interesting exercise, but I would be interested to find out just what type of aircraft can put up this sort of performance!"

1973

North Island's NZSSRG *'Spaceview'* publication contained another interesting report from investigator Vic Harris; *'Capt. Peter Telling, flying a Grand Commander aircraft, at an altitude of ten thousand feet, over the Ohura Beacon area, thought he had a fire in his starboard engine. A fire in an engine on this type of aircraft would be disastrous, he said, so he looked very carefully to assess what was happening.*

'...About thirty yards from the aircraft was a ball of intense bluish-white light, much like a welding arc, that was twenty to forty feet in diameter, and stayed with his aircraft for about twenty to twenty-five seconds. The Automatic Direction-finding Compass, and both the gyroscope compass and magnetic one went haywire, and spun at a speed of about twelve revolutions per minute. All directional equipment remained non-functional until he passed over the Wanganui area. He states that many of his colleagues have had similar experiences, but prefer not to talk about them. His co-pilot is prepared to back his story.'

Peter Telling was best known as Radio I's 'Peter T' and was a pilot three days a week as well as a radio host. He contacted Vic Harris when he was on a talk-back show with Geoff Sinclair in April 1973.

Later, in April 1975 Captain Telling saw a high-flying UFO, changing colours, in the same vicinity.

January 1974

Researcher, Philip Mantle, wrote about Anthony Chatfield, from Renwick, Marlborough, who was an instructor of recruits in the Royal New Zealand Air Force. One warm night he took the cadets outside for some exercise.

Chatfield said; *"After about ten minutes or so, one recruit approached me and asked what it was that was flying along the top of the hills immediately to our north. This is a range of hills called the Richmond Range, and vary in height from about 1,500 feet to 4,500 feet. The distance from RNZAF Woodbourne to the UFO was about six to seven kilometres, but even at that range, it was pretty big. There was no sound, and the object was travelling on a south-westerly direction at, I guess, around 200-250 miles per hour.*

'The best way I can describe the object is that it reminded me of an old-fashioned bar-bell of the type that strongmen used in days gone by. There were two large globes glowing with the same sort of light one sees from a fluorescent light, and they seemed to be joined together by a gold, glowing bar. The light seemed to come from within, and one globe seemed to be smaller than the other, although this could have been due to the angle it was viewed from.'

Visibility was excellent, with a clear sky and some low broken cloud. When the object, which was in view for about three minutes, passed behind a cloud, its light could be seen shining through. Chatfield, who had been an RAF airframe mechanic for five years, noted that this strange craft appeared to have no rudder or fin, no navigation lights and no flashing strobe light. The moon was visible, and he noted that weather balloons do not fly against the wind.

Chatfield added; *"I have spent a lot of time working in and around aircraft, and I can find no logical explanation as to what the object was that I and sixty or so cadets saw. I know full well that the RNZAF had nothing even close to the size of the beast that I saw.*

.... *'About three or four months later, when I was discussing the sighting with a colleague, I went and got the 'Incident Book', that all duty NCOs have to fill in on completion of their tour of duty. I was surprised to discover that the page on which I had recorded the sighting had been removed. I asked about this, but no one could throw light on the matter at all. The page had not been ripped out or torn, but quite neatly cut. What happened to that page I simply do not know. It was shortly after this I discovered that the Civil Aviation Authority had a printed form issued to all Air Traffic Control Centers throughout New Zealand specifically for UFO sightings.'*

Te Kuiti 28th October 1975
At 5am, an engineer, stationed with the Royal New Zealand Navy at Devonport Auckland, noticed a bright white light in the sky over Te Kuiti Aerodrome. After turning a corner, just past Hangataki crossroads, he pulled up to get a better look.

He saw what may have been a second light, but this one was low in the sky, and below it, sitting in a paddock, was a saucer-shaped object, about fifty feet in diameter, with 'one foot' windows all around. He got a bit of a fright, and took off to Auckland, where he was due to report for duty at 8am. As he sped along, he thought the craft, with foggy white lights, was following him down the back road. He lost sight of it after passing through Pirongia.

1st July 1977
'Xenolog' printed a report by an experienced pilot and traffic officer Mark Aronsen who was in a PA 28 (Piper Cherokee) on a short flight in the vicinity of Temuka, South Canterbury:

"I was at an altitude of 7,500feet, and was aware of an inbound F27 Transport plane, and sighted it, about one mile west of my position. It was at 2,000 feet, and on long finals about five miles northwest of Temuka. What caught my attention was the close proximity of a black cigar-shaped object, enveloped in a heat haze, which appeared to be following the F27.

"It was about fifteen metres in length, positioned slightly above the starboard rear of the transport plane, and was maintaining its position at a distance of approximately 400 metres.

"I turned towards the object and commenced a dive in its direction, reaching maximum airframe speed in an effort to intercept it. The UFO stopped dead, hovered for two seconds, then accelerated sharply away on a heading of about 290 degrees magnetic.

"The rate of climb and acceleration was far in excess of anything I have seen before; it was lost to sight within five seconds. In thirteen years of flying I have never seen a craft to compare with that object."

The Kaikoura lights – a major incident

Kaikoura–Wellington, Christmas–New Year 1978–79
This is one of the most discussed and investigated events in ufology. It is a complex series of events, which I will sequence in chronological order. I have used the witness's and participants' real names due to the prior massive publicity these sightings received:

At the end of November/early December, just before the Kaikoura sightings, seven CBers, (citizen radio operators), were up on the Rarangi Hills, making contact with some Wellington CB enthusiasts, who were on the Wellington hills, and overlooking the Straits.

Suddenly, a bright light, the size of a star, appeared in the sky and started to do aerobatics, U-turns and 'figures-of-eight'. This was seen by both sides of the Cook Strait. It then, unexpectedly it started to change colour as it dived towards the sea. It plunged into the water, without making a ripple or any disturbance. It could be seen under the water, emitting a white glow.

Five minutes later, it shot back out of the sea, simultaneously changing colour, and disappeared from view up in the sky. Fearing ridicule from their friends, the seven CBers did not report the incident to the Blenheim authorities.

20th December 1978

Just before midnight air traffic controllers John Cordy and Andy Herd reported "unknown returns" on their radar.

At the same time, at Woodbourne RNZAF Base, Warrant Officer Ian Uffindell saw three bright lights in the southeast sky, near Cape Campbell and the Kaikoura coast. Bill Frame, in the control tower also sighted the white lights – one large, and two smaller, dimmer lights. Bill rang John Cordy, who advised there was no known air traffic to account for them.

During the next hour they moved up and down the coast, hovering at times, with occasional beams of light coming from them at a 45 degree angle. The two smaller objects seemed to move and stop in unison. The police in Blenheim received several calls from the public, and all reports corresponded with the others.

21st December 1978

At 12.50 a.m. Bill Frame, the Flight Services Officer on duty at Woodbourne – Blenheim control tower, was still watching three bright white lights near Cape Campbell. Air Traffic Control at Wellington, picked up a second target – giving a return "the size of a large passenger plane", on radar. It was thirty miles off the coast, southeast of Wellington, and tracked for thirty miles, at about 120 knots, to a point sixty miles east of the mouth of the Clarence River. It then stopped moving for forty-five minutes, and although it has been argued that radar should not pick-up stationary objects, this may not apply to something rotating or spinning. During that time, the Air Traffic Control centre also received a number of calls, reporting strange lights and "weird high-pitched noises" in the area.

At 1.10 a.m. Captain John Randle and First Officer Keith Heine took off from Woodbourne in their four-engine turbo-prop *Argosy* freighter, (SAE – Sierra Alpha Echo), for their regular trip south over Cook Strait, to Christchurch, then back north over Cook Strait and on to Auckland. Air traffic controllers Cordy and Herd asked them to keep a lookout for the objects causing the inexplicable returns.

When they were over Cook Strait, fifteen to twenty miles southwest of Wellington Harbour, the large object was detected moving, at 120 knots some twenty miles towards the *Argosy* track, and stopping again about twenty miles to the east. At the same time the crew, who kept heading south, noted a number of small white lights, close to shore, moving randomly over a considerable distance, occasionally shining down. Their weather radar showed a number of returns of very large objects, the only remote conventional explanation could have been illicit ships, but they would have been dangerously close to shore.

At 3.10 a.m. they left Christchurch for Auckland, and decided to deviate up the coast for another look at the unidentified objects and lights. During their trip up the South Island they saw the smaller lights were over the sea, and not the land, as previously thought. They considered helicopters or boats, but thought it unlikely. When they reached Cape Campbell, the five strong targets faded – then reappeared behind the plane. At the same time, another target was moving in from the east on the same track. At 4.06 a.m., they did an orbit and spotted white lights, with an amber tint, randomly beaming downwards. (There are some differences in the details of witness observations at this time.) The plane proceeded on to Auckland without further incidence.

Simultaneously, at 3.10 a.m., a second *Argosy* plane (SAF – Sierra Alpha Foxtrot) took off from Woodbourne for Christchurch, with Captain Vern Powell and First Officer Ian Pirie in the cockpit. Wellington Radar asked them to also keep a lookout for the radar returns, especially the stationary object to the east of Cape Campbell. When the strange return was fifty miles from SAF, Wellington Radar advised it had moved twenty miles to the west, and halted thirty miles away from the plane, as it had done with the previous SAE flight. Powell could see a bright, glowing white light, tinged with red, but reported it as being a bright red glowing light, about 2,000-3,000 feet above the aircraft. It had been stationary for about forty-five minutes, but then started to move parallel to SAF.

Shortly after 4 a.m. SAF was approaching Christchurch, and another target was detected on the weather radar. It moved one mile closer, now only forty miles away. It put on a burst of incredible speed, heading straight for the plane, before veering left and disappearing off radar. The crew saw very little of this, just a few flashing lights to the front.

Quentin Fogarty, a television journalist in Australia, had returned to New Zealand for the Christmas break, and he was told of the events with the *Argosy* planes by a New Zealand journalist colleague, who asked him to check it out. The recent disappearance of Valentich and his plane over the Bass Strait was still fresh in Fogarty's mind.

He was very interested in the basic scenario that a large target had tracked out from Wellington at 120 knots, moving rapidly towards flight SAE and then made a similar approach to flight SAF, pacing it closely for twelve miles. There were radar, ground and pilot observations, and it was arranged for him to make a news presentation-type documentary.

He contacted David Crockett, a freelance cameraman, and his wife Ngaire, a freelance sound recordist, and together they started interviewing Cordy, Herd, Powell and other witnesses. Powell had commented that he wasn't scared, just excited. He had come to the conclusion that UFOs existed, and if they were going to harm anyone, they would have done so a long time ago.

Quentin wanted to include a re-enactment to complete their footage, and arranged to travel, one way, on a regular *Argosy* newspaper delivery run from Wellington to Christchurch, which covered the same route where both previous planes had encountered the large object.

30th December 1978
At 9.30 p.m. Fogarty's team boarded *Argosy* SAE, with Captain Bill Startup and Flying Officer Bob Guard, and set off on an identical route. It was only intended to be a re-enactment, and Quentin had already recorded the voice-over, "We had no luck in sighting anything mysterious", when the captain called them up to the cockpit.
There was a row of bright pulsating lights hovering over Kaikoura. They contacted Geoff Causer at Wellington Radar, who advised them he had been viewing anomalous targets off the Kaikoura coast for thirty minutes. Due to their erratic nature he had not considered them to be solid. As before, the lights were white to orange pulsating globes, with a red tinge.

31st December 1978
At 12.30 a.m. a second target appeared one mile to their left. It disappeared and then the same, or a third target, with a flashing light, reappeared and hovered, possibly in the same spot, but now three miles away, due to the plane's movement, Wellington Radar was showing a number of targets, which doubled in size for forty-seven seconds, a mile behind and following the plane.

Bill Startup twice performed 360 degree turns, in an attempt to see what was on his tail. The object following them was about four miles away, and looked like a star emitting bright green and white light. Wellington Radar had said the object, on their tail for ten minutes, had now been joined by two others. As they neared Christchurch the target following them, veered away, and headed inland to the southeast.

The film crew had only intended to make a one-way trip to Christchurch, but knew something was going on up there, and since they had obtained very little footage, Bill Startup invited them to make the return journey to Blenheim. Ngaire Crockett was very nervous about taking the return trip, and New Zealand Television journalist Dennis Grant took her place.

Only two minutes after take-off, at 2.15am, while they were still climbing through the cloud, they saw a bright light, just within twenty miles on radar, keeping track with them. They cleared the cloud ten miles out of Christchurch, and observed a very bright, round yellowish-white light above, which was lighting up the surrounding clouds.

As they were going up the coast they could see a "great big" target at 3 o'clock and an altitude of 11,500 feet. David Crockett was in the cockpit filming as much as possible. He later told Harvey Cooke that he was having to move from one side of the cockpit to the other, and at times was leaning over the co-pilot's shoulder to get photos below, to the right, and then upwards or to the left. The strange object, in fast erratic movements, stayed with the plane, going ahead, then in front, across then away underneath.

Through his lens, Crockett could detect a definite structure through the light. It looked like a traditional flying saucer, with a brightly lit bottom and a transparent sphere on top. At times, through the camera, it appeared to be as large as a three storey building.

Christchurch Radar was turned off, and Wellington Radar advised the *Argosy* that were out of range, but they did have lots of targets off Clarence, north of Kaikoura. The object had been following them for about 10-12 minutes. They were thirty-five miles out of Christchurch, at 13,000 feet, when Startup took the plane off autopilot and made a 90-degree turn towards the target, putting it in front of the plane. The object moved to the right, indicating some form of intelligent control.

It now moved to the front and below the plane, and then picked up speed and came back straight up towards the plane. In the footage it looked like a grey-white oval shape craft with rings of light going around.

Before they landed back in Blenheim at 3.30 a.m. on the 31st December, there was a lot more activity recorded visually and on radar. Going towards the North Island the aircraft picked up radar returns consistent with Wellington Radar and visual sightings.

Heading towards Kaikoura East, Startup thought he saw a second object ahead and above the aircraft. Flying into Cape Campbell a huge bright light – orange with a red tinge, came into view high above Blenheim. The plane banked for landing, and they lost sight of it.

Dave Crockett said that when the aircrew landed at Blenheim, they were so upset and scared that they just left the aircraft immediately, and forgot to unload the newspapers. They had to make an effort to go back and do so.

There was much excitement all round. Quentin Fogarty and the footage were raced back to Melbourne and Channel 0 late on 31st December. He had to work on getting it ready to go to air, and there were problems over copyright and use of the film. Eventually, after nearly three days without sleep, he was close to physical and mental collapse, and had to take three days off, returning to work on 5th January 1979.

For a long time afterwards Quentin Fogarty was exposed to extreme harassment, from sceptics, lunatics and even his own employers. A lot of inaccurate and incomplete data was publicised in the media. (I met Quentin while in Melbourne, and found him to be a quiet, modest, intelligent and very honourable man. In 1982 he wrote the book 'Let's Hope They're Friendly!' I can recommend it as an exceptionally good example of the unpleasant and unethical practices that permeate the entire ufology scene, and victimise honest witnesses such as Quentin.)

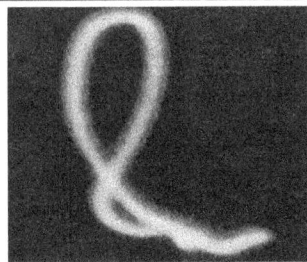

This famous frame from the film may show a UFO travelling at 18,000 metres per second

About two days after the story made headlines, the New Zealand Air Force sent up an Orion with sophisticated monitoring equipment. They said they didn't find anything and suggested some unspecified, unusual natural phenomena. Their conclusion was couched in slightly ambiguous terms as it said it was not a craft from an unfriendly nation and of no defence significance.

However, on 2nd January, *'The Sun'* newspaper claimed that *'A strike squadron of RNZAF Skyhawk fighter-bombers is on standby to intercept the UFOs if possible.'* The next day, the *'Daily Mirror'* sported even more spectacular headlines; *'Warplane Chases UFOs for Five Hours – An Air Force tracker aircraft chased mystery UFO radar blips over New Zealand for five hours until early today. But the strange contacts on New Zealand ground radar disappeared every time the RNZAF plane gave chase.'*

The film footage and details of the encounters were sent to the USA by Channel 0. They were examined by over twenty scientists, and experts in radar, optics and physics, and included:

- Bruce Maccabee, US Navy Surface Weapons Centre
- John Acuff, President *'NICAP'*
- Professor Allen Hynek, Director *'CUFOS'*
- Dr. Gilbert Levin, Biophysicist
- Dr. Peter Sturrock, Plasma Physicist, Stanford
- Dr. Richard Haines, Optical Physiologist, NASA

They commented that it was the only UFO sighting at the time, which had radar, visual and photographic evidence, and couldn't be identified by conventional means. They all ruled out the explanations proffered by authorities, sceptics, armchair critics, and other self-proclaimed experts.

The phenomenon was not – Venus, Jupiter, stars, meteorites, ball lightning, aeroplanes, ground lights, fishing boats, cabin light reflections, migrating mutton birds, reflections off cabbage patches, and certainly not a hoax or any of the other explanations which attempted to sweep the whole matter under the carpet.

(All of the witnesses were adamant that none of these explanations added up. Two of them remarked; "I've never seen a squid boat 13,000 feet up in the air", and "I'd like to know who is growing cabbages twenty miles out of the south-east of Wellington, well over the sea!")

They commented that no conventional object behaved that way, and while they had ruled out all other explanations and reasons, they couldn't totally eliminate Russian or American secret flying machines. They noted that Nazi Germany had plans for such craft as early as 1941, and the United States' *'flying flapjack'* which had never reached fruition.

In New Zealand, one pilot suggested they were experiments in holographic target decoys or interferometry by the Australian and New Zealand Navies. Another man claimed he had worked with top-secret Air Force projects – 'Hookdown' and 'Sidescan', involving controlled drones, and that the Americans had been testing advanced drones on Civil Aviation radar.

Bruce Cathie, a New Zealand airline pilot and ufologist, believed the objects were both man-made and extraterrestrial drawing their energy source from a world-wide grid system. He claimed a world-wide group of scientists had combined their research into one major experiment, based on re-engineering craft from outer space.

Quentin Fogarty does not hold an extraterrestrial theory, and felt that while they were intelligent, they may be something other than physical reality as we understand it.

In an article for *'BUFORA'* he wrote; *'Once in a while, there is a case which stands up to scrutiny. Such an event occurred in the early morning of December 31st, 1978, off New Zealand's South Island, when a television crew saw and filmed a number of bright airborne lights. The case was investigated by American optical physicist, Dr. Bruce Maccabee, a consultant for 'NICAP'. He referred his findings to twenty fellow scientists and experts in radar, optics and physics, who agreed that the light sources defied logical explanation. The film was declared the first verified movie footage of a UFO.*

'As one of the passengers of that flight, I too, suffered at the hands of the debunkers. I have been called many things since the encounter – hoaxer, liar, fool, even the George Adamski of the 1980s. The scoffing increased when two days after the sighting, I collapsed from the pressure of overwork and lack of sleep, and was admitted to hospital.

(As soon as he had landed in Blenheim, Channel 0 ordered Fogarty back to Melbourne with the film. – *'We worked all night, putting our film together... I sat down at a typewriter and tried to write the scripts. My head was spinning, and at 8am, I had to be helped to an office where two couches had been put together to make a bed. I put my head down and was out like a light. It had been fifty long, sleepless hours.*

'I admit to only one major failing – naivety. When I told my incredible story, it did not occur to me that people would disbelieve it. After all, I had seen the

things with my own eyes, as had the others on board, including the pilot, a man with twenty-four years flying experience. More important, the objects had been tracked on radar.)

One of Quentin's supporters, Paul Norman from '*VUFORS*', took a shot at the debunkers when he wrote; *'One of the most amusing suggestions came from an ornithologist.... 'Mutton birds flying inland for mating'. If true, it would have been a great day for students of ornithology, because it was the first recorded appearance of supersonic mutton birds, which were, for some unknown reason, in great haste to get on with the job. Clocked at five miles per second, this strong species of seagull would surely have been equipped with asbestos feathers!'*

Sceptics conveniently ignored the fact that witnesses has reported other UFO sightings in the last week of December, and many reports were received from up and down the country in the first week of the New Year.

In late January, New Zealand's Prime Minister, and the Leader of the Opposition saw an object pacing the plane they were in as they passed over Kaikoura at 9pm. It was tracked on the plane's and Wellington's radar.

There was also a more sinister side to this whole episode. New Zealander, Bill Startup had taken some important film footage of the 'Kaikoura Lights', seen from the plane at the end of 1978. Later, he visited the home of fellow witness, David Crockett, in Island Bay, Wellington, to show him the documentary film he had just made. Just after, Crockett's home was mysteriously burned down. Fortunately, the film was not there at the time, and it is not known if this event prompted the Crockett's decision to move to Hawaii.

White Death 1979

Most of us are aware of the frantic transmissions by Frederick Valentich in 1978, when he claimed contact with a UFO before he and his plane mysteriously disappeared over Bass Strait. In late 1979 an Air New Zealand DC-10 tragically crashed into Mt Erebus during a sightseeing flight to the Antarctic.

A few days later I received a long-distance call from John Pinkney, a Victorian researcher and journalist. He claimed he had information from several ham radio operators, in Australia and New Zealand, that just before the plane crashed they had picked up a distress message stating it was being buzzed by a craft of unknown shape and origin.

I am still not sure if John was seeking further information, or just wanted my opinion. My thoughts immediately turned to a case in Madrid, a couple of weeks before. Several UFOs had pursued a passenger plane, which had made an emergency landing at the airport. My initial comment was, "They missed the Madrid plane, but grabbed one over the Antarctic instead!"

I revised that opinion later, when the official investigation determined that the plane was on the wrong course and headed straight for the mountain. I wondered if the UFO had disrupted the plane's instruments. Perhaps the unidentified craft was trying to warn them they were on the wrong course? We will never know.

I advised John he would never be able to publish this information, and felt sure the authorities would prevent it one way or another, if only for the tired old reason of 'not frightening the public'. John was so convinced of the accuracy of the reports that he swore he would publish and be damned. He did and probably was.

In December, 1979, the 'Melbourne Truth' published his article where he stated his informants were senior RAAF officers and public servants, and the UFO messages were received in both Auckland and Sydney. Air traffic controllers and RAAF personnel were ordered to keep the UFO report top secret. The RAAF and NZAF were placed on full alert following the crash.

The Department of Transport denied any radio transmissions about unusual objects. John commented, "If any UFO evidence is found in the DC10's flight deck recording or in the black box, you can be sure it will never be publicly released."

In February 1980, John wrote in the 'Daily Mirror' that two contacts had premonitions of the crash. However, they had said nothing because they did not have enough accurate details, and thought they would be ridiculed and ignored:

One Sydney woman had a dream that she was floating alongside a plane which took off from an airport. She saw it descend rapidly into a big white mass and explode. She woke in fright, feeling somehow it was more than a dream.

Another gentleman described a 'vision', after he got an enormous pain in his nose, while changing his car tyre. He thought he'd been hit by something, "but then realised the pain was in my mind. It didn't stop me seeing stars, but then something else – a vivid vision of a plane hitting a steep white wall. The vision was so intense I had no trouble recognising the crash mountain when it appeared on television several days later."

Blenheim 14th July 1980

The *'Marlborough Express'* reported that at about midnight, when Mr. Campbell-Board opened a window in his home, to let the cat out, he saw a bright, white light over Blenheim, moving horizontally in a north-east direction. The night was clear, and no sound of an aircraft could be heard. He and his wife stood on the terrace, and watched it veer slightly to the right and move steadily towards some pine trees.

They rang the Woodbourne control tower, who said there were no planes in the area. The Controller, D. McManus, recorded the frequency of unaccounted 'blips', then rang Wellington Radar, who said at 12.05am the object was on their screen, moving to the north-east. The sighting was 'unaccounted for', as there were no aircraft reported or scheduled at the time.

Southland 12th June 1981

It became apparent, that by the 1980's, some authorities just didn't want to know about UFOs and the subsequent publicity and media attention, no matter if a witness had some expertise in aviation.

On 16th June 1981, the Christchurch press published the following report; *'Two more persons have told the police that they had seen a UFO on Friday evening. "First reports of the object reportedly seen near Wyndham, have come from a Forest Service Ranger and the pilot of a light aircraft'," said Constable J. Reid of Wyndham.*

*'The object was said to be 'long and tear-shaped with several white lights along the side". The Ranger told Constable Reid that he had seen the object at 5.30pm, and that it 'Sparked like a child's fireworks sparkler'. It was moving north quickly, with a slight downward trajectory, before disappearing behind trees. **Constable Reid said he had not spoken to the pilot, nor was he likely to!'***

Apparently, since the sky was clear, and it was only just starting to get dark, the media were relying on a possible investigation by the Civil Aviation Division at Christchurch.

Waikato and Bay of Islands 25th February 1995

Suzy Hanson and Graeme Opie, wrote about two balls of light, one green and one reddish/orange, which were seen by Suzy, at 10.30pm., descending from the sky toward Mayor Island.

Some days later, at 1.17pm on 9th March, a similar object was seen moving from the sea, in an east to westerly direction, towards the coastline. It passed over Motiti Island, towards Papamoa on the coast, before rising over the Kaimai Ranges towards the Waikato. One of the several witnesses, a qualified meteorologist, described it as being a bright silver, metallic, sphere-like object, surrounded by a pinkish-orange, halo-type 'bow wave'.

The same day, at 1,20pm, Air Traffic Control at Hamilton and Rotorua Airports received three calls reporting an unusual object, with a long 'tail', travelling from east to west towards Hamilton. Graeme Opie, the Senior Air traffic Controller at Hamilton Airport, looked out of the window, and could see the strange craft, to the south, and still maintaining an east to west course. It had a 'shiny head' and was travelling very fast, at least the speed of a 'jet fighter'.

Experts ruled out the possibility of a meteorite or fireball, and Auckland ATC Radar Centre, said that there were no aircraft in these areas at the time.

Air Traffic Controller, Graeme Opie said; *"I consider that what I saw from the control tower was a UFO –definitely some form of controlled UFO/craft. Very interesting that it did not appear on our radar screens."*

Sometimes, details of an event can be tantalizingly out of reach. In 1976, during a *'Sunday Best'* program on Wellington's TV2, a NAC pilot recounted how he and his captain, during a 1969 regular flight from Wellington to Nelson, had seen a blue UFO. It was flying slowly, well below them, at an altitude of about 3,000ft, in a south-westerly direction, and was last seen by other airline pilots moving west beyond Cape Campbell.

Of course, seven years after the incident, it was nigh impossible to follow up on any other meaningful details.

CHAPTER SIX

THE 1970s

By the 1970s, multiple reports were flooding in of strange lights and craft in the sky. Whilst, by that time, the military and commercial interests would have been experimenting with secret prototypes, it was unlikely that there would have been so many, or that they would have been tested in New Zealand, a relatively small country, with no uninhabited desert areas, the normal venue for clandestine operations.

Mount Cook (Aoraki)

In the 1970s Jason was a porter at the Hermitage Hotel below Mount Cook (Aoraki). During one evening he noticed a green, red and orange ball of bright light down in the valley below, near Lake Pukaki. He had a look with his binoculars, as it seemed unusual and was pulsating. He went on with his work, and checked half an hour later, at about 10 p.m., when it was still in the same position.

"I lost interest and retired to the staff quarters. The following week I had a couple of days off. I finished work at about 5 p.m. and was about to head to my parents' home in Timaru, a four-hour drive. I was in a hurry, as it was mid-winter and it got dark early. I was halfway there, at about 7 p.m., and between Lake Tekapo and the township of Fairlie when my 1951 Ford V8 Twin Spinner started missing and surging. I was worried, because I had just had a new fuel pump installed, and I thought it was failing.

"I was looking at the car's gauges, when out of the corner of my eye, through the passenger window, I saw that same ball of light. At the same time my engine cut out, and I put my foot on the clutch so that it would coast along down the hill. Luckily my headlights still worked.

"The light was now a huge sphere, the size of a basketball, with red, green, orange and yellow colours mingling and merging, quite brilliant in the clear, dark starry sky. It seemed to be following me, keeping pace with my car, like it was playing with me. I thought, 'shall I pull over and stop? No, better to coast along.' At this stage it silently passed behind my car, and I was getting very nervous as this seemed to go on for a very long time.

"Suddenly it picked up speed, turned gracefully in front of my car, and sped back off high into the southeast sky at phenomenal speed. I breathed a sigh of relief, and let out the clutch. The engine started again. It ran trouble free for the rest of my journey – at a fast pace, I might add!"

Jason has tried to think of more conventional explanation, noting that the McKenzie Basin area is full of hydro-electric dams and long lines of power pylons, supplying the national grid.

He also noted that there is an Astronomical Observatory at Mt. John, next to Lake Tekapo. This is run by Canterbury University Physics Department in Christchurch, in association with the Lick Observatory (University of California, United Sates). Besides the usual range of astronomical functions, the observatory conducts sky-mapping and satellite tracking for the United States Air Force, via the University of California.

Christchurch 1st February 1970

'SACTU' reported that Mr. Morris and his family were staying at the Aranui Motel and Holiday Camp, and at about 10.55pm, when he was about to get into his sleeping bag, he saw an unusual, elongated object travelling in the sky, at high speed towards the west. He could only see the underside of the craft, but likened it to 'a flattened curling stone with no handle'. He said it was massive, and appeared to be solid, like an ocean liner from a low angle.

He wasn't sure if anyone would believe him, but a friend, who was an amateur astronomer, said that at about the same time, N.A.C. pilots and Radar in Wellington had reported something similar.

Waitakeri Ranges 23rd February 1970

W. Murray saw some strange lights over towards the Waitakeri Ranges, and when they descended below the peaks, he and a friend went to the top of Mt. Pukematakeo 'to see if there was anything to see'!

Arriving at the summit, they observed at least ten lights swooping and weaving just above the tree tops. In order to get a better view, they drove down the road to a spot which looked out over Henderson Valley, and were astounded to see, hovering below, a large disc, about sixty metres in diameter, with a dark sphere on top. They took fright, and raced home as quickly as possible.

The next night, after curiosity had overcome his fear, he ventured back alone, as his friend was too scared to join him. When he reached the same spot, he could see a few unusual lights. After about five minutes, two of the lights 'wobbled' closer, followed by a dark, saucer- shape, which appeared and slowly 'hovered' towards him. He took off, and sped away faster than he had the first time.

Half a mile down the road, he thought the object was following him, so he abandoned his car and raced on foot to a nearby house. Before hastily shutting the door, the startled residents agreed he could shelter outside until he felt it was safe to go back to his car.

Auckland 30th April 1970

Tony Brunt, along with another '*NZSSRG*' investigator, spoke to Mrs. Sutherland, at Whitford, who woke at 4.30am, and made a cup of tea, as there was no need to milk the cows, who were usually 'dry' at that time of year. Her home was situated on an elevated position, with an uninterrupted view of the surrounding countryside. Through the window, she could see a brightly lit object descending slowly from the sky, over a neighbour's paddock, about a mile away in a north-easterly direction.

It was about thirty feet high, flat and oval-shaped, with a 'cylinder-like thing' rising from the centre, the top being like the neck and shoulders of a round bottle. This portion was orange, the body of the oval shape was pink and the lower portion orange. As the object was turning, an enormous, brilliant light came into focus, and illuminated everything around. She noted there appeared to be three 'V' shapes below the craft, with three 'inverted Vs on top of them, creating three forms somewhat resembling squares at an angle along the bottom of the craft. Around the whole object was a circle of soft, green luminous light, with another circle of pink lying outside it. These colours were clearly defined, and the whole object was clear and brilliantly lit.

She watched for about thirty minutes, as the object moved slowly and silently over the countryside before disappearing into a gully.

Maraenui – Napier 7th May 1970

'*The Napier Daily Telegraph*' reported that on May 7th, for over twenty minutes, the headmaster, teachers and more than 400 children at Richmond School, Maraenui, watched a brilliantly lit, saucer-shaped object, which initially appeared iridescent, and resembled a 'hole in the sky', which was clear at the time. One of the teachers, Mr. Billings, said that it was like a huge, wingless plane, - a solid metallic object, an elongated oval shape, with the sun glistening on it, however it was also glistening on the side away from the sun.

The object appeared to be hovering between Westshore and Tongoio, and after three or four minutes, it began to move away at right-angles, then increased speed and shot away out of sight.

Mr. Billings said; "We thought half of Napier would have seen it. Here, at the school, everyone was standing with their mouths open, trying to work out a logical answer to it. When a pupil came up and asked me it it was a flying saucer, I said "yes", because I couldn't give any other answer."

Auckland 16th November 1970

The 'Auckland Star' reported that three members of the Remuera, Goodwin family, saw a strange object in the sky at 6.30pm one evening. Their neighbour, Mrs. Young, also independently witnessed the same event.

When Deborah first saw the craft it was coming closer and inland, then it stopped, and seemed to be suspended in the air, before moving again, but this time in an up and down motion.

Ray Goodwin said; "My daughter first pointed out the object in the sky, which I dismissed as an aeroplane. On further looking, I could see it wasn't an aeroplane usually observed. It appeared dark brown in colour, with portholes of light on its leading edge. The object moved at great speed and manoeuvred in a manner impossible for ordinary flying machines. When it turned on its side it was circular and about forty to sixty feet across."

Mrs. Goodwin likened it to an enormous golden cigar-shape object, with dark patches. She said it continued to come closer, then dropped and came back up with great speed and did a series of angle movements. Then it made a long, angular sweep, at which time it showed a pure oval shape.

Ray, along with his wife and daughter, watched it for about twenty-five minutes, until it seemed to quickly descend towards the edge of the Tamaki Estuary, and was lost from sight in the background of trees and houses.

Taupo 15th April 1971

The '*Taupo Times*' interviewed two men – Roger Morel and Robin Hay, who at 9pm on 15th April, were returning home to Taupo after completing their forestry duties. Earlier they had noticed their pig-dog had become agitated for no apparent reason.

Five miles out of town, they stopped to check their tail light, and over the caravan park and camp site, saw huge object hovering overhead. It had a base the size of a 'Friendship' aircraft, and was shaped like a 'Mexican hat'. There were flickering orange and yellow lights, which appeared to be revolving; '*A band of yellow lights showed half-way to the top, and the body itself was a hazy green, with a metallic sheen.*'

For about ten minutes, while they watched, they left their vehicle engine switched off. When they drove on towards Taupo, which was about five miles away, they thought it may have been following them, but they lost sight of it after passing through the cutting west of the De Brett Thermal Hotel.

Arthur's Pass 18th June 1971

At 11.30 pm., four university students, who were part of a work-party, had driven up from Christchurch. They were walking up a track to a hut on the Temple Basin ski-fields, when they saw a very bright object to the left of, and above, Mt. Bealey, approximately five to six miles away. It was a cool, clear night, with the stars visible.

It caught their attention because it was moving erratically, both vertically and horizontally – 'somewhat like a great horizontal yo-yo'. They watched it for over an hour, before it made a series of sweeping movements back and forth over Arthurs Pass Township. They were startled when it suddenly came closer, about half a mile away, and they could see a distinct saucer shape, about twenty feet in diameter, with a white light on top. It appeared to have a powerful white light in the centre, which was rotating extremely fast. As its speed increased, so did the light intensity. To their relief, the strange craft then reversed, banked and silently shot off in a south to south-east direction and not seen again.

Rotorua 3rd July 1971

A young lady and her boyfriend went to the Saturday night movies, and after a short drive, bought some hamburgers and parked at the lakeside. After they had stayed there, until about 1.45am, and when the other cars had left, they heard a loud noise, and looked out the window. Over the water, they could see an object, which looked like a light-grey/white inverted plate with a small darker grey dome on the top.

There was a fog around the base of the object, so they couldn't tell if it was floating or hovering. Set off-centre of the dome was a bright red light, which rotated clockwise, and seemed more intense when pointed towards their car window. At the same time, a metallic-sounding beep could be heard. The frequency of both the 'beep' and the light was about once per second.

They estimated the craft as being about thirty to forty feet wide at the base, the dome as being about two feet high, and the entire craft at about ten to fifteen feet at its highest point. After about four minutes, they started the car, and proceeded, at some speed, losing sight of the strange craft after a short time.

Waihi 2nd September 1971

At 3.30pm. a young newspaper boy, delivering the afternoon newspapers, was startled when he saw a round, grey object flying in a circle, at a low altitude, near the railway line. At times it appeared oval, and others more of a 'hat shape'. After three or four minutes, it shot away in the direction of Tauranga.

Otorohanga 3rd/4th September 1971

After *'Civilian Aerial Phenomena Research'* investigated an incident in 1971, Phil Ackman, a reporter from the local Hamilton newspaper couldn't resist publishing the following account; *'Oterchanga police are searching for a little green man carrying a 14-foot shovel and about half a ton of dirt. And if their suspect seems unbelievable, he's no more unbelievable than the fourteen-foot-deep hole which has mysteriously appeared in a local farm. Of course, the 'little green man' concept is only Oterchanga police humour. He could just as easily be a psychedelic purple or bright red, one police officer pointed out. But, whatever colour he is, he's certainly the only suspect, so far unearthed, for the sinister hole-digging crime.'*

This strange scenario had apparently occurred on more than one property. The first victims were a local farmer, Mr. Shields, and his share milker, Mr. Singh. On the night of the 3rd/4th September, they saw an orange object pass across the sky. It was smaller than the moon, but its bright halo was enough to obscure the moon and a bright planet nearby. It accelerated, changing to a brilliant white, stopped at about thirty degrees above the horizon, and then rose vertically and disappeared. They went to bed, and heard nothing that night. Further their dogs didn't appear to have been disturbed.

The next day, they noticed a hole, a foot wide and fourteen feet deep, only 100ft to 120ft away from a homestead, and exactly mid-way between two fences on their 'cattle race' property. They were at a loss to explain it, as the ground was too muddy and inaccessible for a tractor or drilling apparatus. The green turf around the top had been clearly cut, and they pointed out that whoever dug the hole would have needed a very long shovel. Further, what had they done with the dirt, which it was estimated would have been 400 – 500lbs?

The police said they weren't even sure they wanted to catch the culprit, as besides other considerations, *'they couldn't be too sure what to charge him with'*.

Despite hilarity on the part of the press, the 'Otorohanga Hole' did exist, and experts from *'SACTU'* were visiting the scene to investigate. They verified that the hole was in fact nine inches wide and fifteen feet deep, with a second hole only two feet away and one foot deep. They were located, within a three feet radius, in a muddy area, with no footprints to be seen. They confirmed that the area was extremely muddy and inaccessible, and the 'holes' had smooth sides right down, as if made by a rotating tool. No machine in the area was capable of doing that, and further, no crawler or tractor marks were evident.

Multiple soil samples were tested. One expert stated that; 'the mud had been originally heated – definitely over 400° C, and probably less than 800° C.' He suggested that there was 'something strange' or unusual about the one sample, however, the cause of this anomaly, or its perpetrators, was never discovered.

Tairua about 1972
In 1977, Harvey Cooke wrote to Fred and Phyllis Dickeson, and in his letter, mentioned a sighting which had occurred about five years earlier. Apparently, a deep sea fisherman and his companion were out in his launch, about six miles east of Great Barrier Island. Dawn had just broken when they saw a disc-like object rise out of the sea some distance ahead. The water in that spot is about 600ft deep. After ascending a short height, the craft moved in the direction of his boat, before speeding away at about 2,000 mph.

Auckland 29th January 1972

'*NZSSRG*' on the North Island, interviewed five school children saw a strange object about 100 yards away in the dusk sky. It was about 7.45pm, and they were resting after playing a game of ball-tag.

They saw a shape, like an upturned saucer, over a neighbour's pine tree. It had one white flashing light in the front, a green one at the rear, and a red light flashing at the top of the dome. When they climbed onto a swing, to get a better look, they noticed that the craft had three portholes on the dome, and five on the base. It was thought to be about thirty feet long and ten feet high.

They watched it for about five minutes. It was moving very slowly towards Milford, then dropped, supposedly towards Lake Pupuke or the Milford shopping area, when it was lost from sight.

Kelston, Auckland 24th May 1972

At about 6.45am, Michael Poninghouse went outside to get his brother's schoolbag from the front lawn, and saw a 'thing' in the sky. He noticed that it was about 'half the size of a football field', (sixty yards), clearly outlined with a flat bottom and curved top, and bluish in colour, with yellow streaks.

Underneath were a 'whole lot of lights', which seemed to be going into the bottom of larger craft. Before he took the bag back into the house, Michael stood and watched the unusual 'thing', which had moved over nearby High School.

He realised that there was some kind of 'door' in the centre of the object's flat bottom, and the dull, red disc shaped lights were still milling around underneath it. He counted about ten of them as they seemed to enter the larger craft by way of the 'door'. The object and surrounding discs eventually moved across the Waikumete Cemetery towards the Waitakeres and disappeared in the distance.

Lower Hutt July 1972

By 1972, it was more probable that some craft were of more earthly origin. One clear July night that year, a woman in Lower Hutt, was in her second-storey bedroom, unable to get to sleep. At 2am she noticed that the area outside her open window was turning a peculiar blue colour. The light, which was accompanied by a sound like a 'spinning top', intensified until the whole room lit up.

She got up, went to the window, and then froze with fear. Hovering over the neighbouring block of flats was a strange craft, about thirteen feet in diameter, and shaped like an inverted soup plate. It appeared to be bluish-grey metal, with a clear dome on top, and flame coloured lights under the outer rim.

The object seemed to be was suspended mid-air, and she could clearly see two figures inside. They looked like normal human males, and were wearing shining light blue satin-type suits, but no helmets. She could only see their heads and shoulders, and the arms of one who was apparently controlling the craft.

The being on the far side of the dome turned to the other who had his back to the witness. He said something, and then laughed. After hovering for a short while, the craft suddenly shot straight up into the air and disappeared south-west over the Wainuiomata Hill.

The witness was so scared that the strange object and occupants may return, rather than notify anyone, she climbed back into bed, and pulled the blankets over her head.

Hastings 19th February 1973

At about 11.30pm several people in various parts of the area, reported a 'huge', bright yellow and red, luminous cigar-shaped object, which travelled north before disappearing behind Flagstaff Hill. It appeared to have a ball of fire following behind it, and one witness, who was a professional engineer and amateur astronomer, calculated its speed as being at least 1,800 mph.

South Auckland 5th October 1973

At 11.30pm, Bill Van der Vegte and his wife, who had been to the Auckland Boat Show, were nearing their home in Karaka, when they noticed what they assumed was a flare in the sky. As they pulled into their driveway, they realised the light was getting closer, so Bill went back out into the road to get a better view.

He could see a 'bell' or 'hat-shaped' object, with multi-coloured lights, and what looked like windows on the side. As it moved, at about twenty miles per hour, towards the silos on Butland's Experimental Farm, Bill called to his wife to come and witness what he was seeing.

The object, which was about twenty-five feet across, was hovering, noiselessly, fifty feet above the silos, displaying a distinct 'up and down' motion. It moved over, towards some trees, before disappearing behind a hill.

Auckland 1974

'*UFORAN's*' New Zealand correspondent, John Knapman, wrote; '*During the early part of 1974, residents around the Hunua Ranges, south of Auckland, many of them too embarrassed to give their names, reported numerous sightings of what they claimed were disc or cone-shaped objects giving off extremely bright light. Over the same period, Wellsford residents, north of Auckland, also made similar sightings.*

'*In the Dome Valley area, near Wellsford, Mr. Eric Marks claimed to have seen, from close quarters, a huge 'craft', about one hundred feet across. He said it looked like a plate with a dome on top, and appeared to be suspended above the ground on 'pencil-like rays'. This description tallies with many others from over the years, both in New Zealand and abroad.*

'*An ex-Merchant Navy officer, who is a trained navigator, spotted what seemed to be a similar craft hovering over Mana Island, near Wellington, in 1958. He watched it with disbelief for a while before it took off vertically at terrific speed.*'

Hamilton 21st April 1974

The Dickesons reported on four witnesses who were travelling along the highway, near Te Uku, when they saw a few flashes of light which seemed to be coming from a particular point in the sky.

They looked more carefully, and realised that there was an object there, below the ridge, and at an altitude of about two hundred feet. It initially only appeared as a round, flat shadow, however, when it became illuminated, they could see it was round-shaped, with a complete circle around the middle. It seemed to be the 'circle' which was lighting up, sending flashes of light to the ground below. Although it was a very large craft – 'about the size of a tennis court' – it was travelling very slowly to the east, before turning and moving south before disappearing from sight.

Yaldhurst 1975

New Zealand researcher, Bryan Dickeson, told me of an unusual case Prudence Buttery had unearthed after an interview with a local woman.

In 1975, at 6.30am, Mary was driving to work, along Buchanans Road, Yaldhurst. She noticed a huge sphere approaching from across the fields on her right. It was wider than her car, and had a turquoise blue centre, and a white aura all around.

She wasn't afraid, just puzzled. She backed up three times, but the object seemed to be following, as if observing her. In her mind she was asking; "What are you, and what do you want?"

Eventually it moved over the road and into a field of cabbages, finally disappearing from sight. She was nearly half an hour late for work, but doesn't know why, and didn't think much of it at the time.

Two weeks later, she was working in her front garden at 7am one morning, when she heard a voice saying; "Can I speak to you?"

She stepped onto the drive where a man, just over six feet tall, was standing. It was a hot summer day, but he was dressed in common farm working clothes of herringbone serge. He was wearing long pants, a trench coat, scarf, gloves and a wide brim hat.

He showed her a drawing of a red sphere, and asked her if she had seen it? Mary told him the sphere she had seen was blue, and she didn't think anyone else had seen it. She said he could ask at the Yaldhust hotel when it opened later that morning. He moved away, and wanting to ask more, she looked over the hedge. He was gone - no car, no bike, nothing!

In front of her property was a four kilometre open side road leading to the main thoroughfare. She told her husband about the two events, but he just laughed. Three weeks later the local newspaper printed a story about a cylindrical 'mother-ship' above the airport near Yaldhurst. It was seen by other people, and had smaller spheres going in and out.

Auckland 8th January 1975

A young couple at Manurewa were returning from a fishing trip, when they noticed a light approaching them from a paddock on their right. It was a strange circular object with a bright white transparent dome, and four lights around the rim. Underneath were four 'legs', each with a red light on it. Sheryl became very frightened when it followed them, for over half a mile. At times it was only twenty feet above their vehicle, when she could see what appeared to be three shadowy figures moving inside. Dale pulled into the nearest driveway, and the craft, which was making a soft humming sound, hovered for a few seconds before shooting off over the hills.

Tauranga 27th May 1975

Researcher, Harvey Cooke, reported that at 2pm, all the children, along with their teacher, at Bellevue School, watched for ten minutes as a red Fletcher-type plane, followed by a UFO, travelled from north to south across the sky. (It was later ascertained that the plane had been practising instrument flying, over Tauranga, at the time).

Both objects appeared to be the size of a car seen at the same distance, however the UFO was a chrome colour, cigar-shaped, slightly curved on top and flat underneath. It was bright and shiny, both ends rounded, and the stern finer than its nose. It had no vapour trail, wings or tail, and no apparent portholes or windows.

The strange object moved along behind the plane at a slightly slower speed, and seemed to follow the plane when it veered off into cloud. The plane suddenly manoeuvred behind a cloud, and flew back in the opposite direction, upon which the UFO hovered, then dived steeply a short distance, before tipping sharply upwards and disappearing from sight about four times the speed of the plane.

Harvey also noted that; *'When the plane was over one of the fields, containing five horses, they showed no interest, but when the UFO hovered in the same place, the clustered horses appeared to panic, at first facing uphill, looking at the object, then rearing and taking off downhill at full gallop.'*

Dome Valley 16th August 1975

Investigator Vic Harris reported on this incident, which occurred at 11.30pm at Windy Ridge, Warkworth.

Mrs. Cook stopped her car, and along with her two daughters, got out to stare at a strange craft which had been travelling south towards Auckland before moving swiftly towards them as they were driving down the road.

It was hovering about a mile away, and appeared to have a long, oval section, about the size of a Toyota van, 'upturned on end'. Mrs. Cook described it as being a bluish-white colour, whilst one daughter said it had a green, flashing light, changing to gold, and having a faint vapour trail. Her other daughter thought the long, oval object was surrounded by blue-white luminous lights, pointing downwards.

After hovering in the one spot, the silent object moved closer to the witnesses, and briefly hovered about 100 yards away. It then took off, at a terrific speed, south towards Auckland.

Tokoroa 1976

'*NZSSRG*' reported on how Reg Scouse went outside his house, to put his bike away, when he noticed a 'most weird- looking object' in the sky. He called out to his mother, and they both watched for five minutes before it silently moved towards the forest and vanished into the dark hills.

It resembled the common description as being similar to a hat with a round brim. There were white vertical lines on the upper section of the craft, which had an orangey-red light on top. The bottom portion was also white, and had several large red lights, rotating very fast, in a clockwise direction.

Reg said that it couldn't have been an aircraft, due to its shape, however he didn't contact the authorities because, despite his mother's presence, they may have thought he imagined the whole thing. (Already it was common practise to 'down-play' any reports.)

Palmerston North 24th June 1976

Harold Fulton submitted the following account to '*Xenolog*'; '*.....at 3.30pm Mrs. Mary Watson, and her two teenage daughters, Gail 16 and Karen 15, were at home in Palmerston North, when Gail chanced to look out the kitchen window. Facing south, low in the sky, were three silvery – seemingly rotating circular objects, flying in a triangular formation. Very startled, she pointed them out to her sister, and called her mother.*

'The three watched the extraordinary trio swoop below the low cloud, heading from east to west. The objects, with an apparent diameter larger than the disc of the full moon, disappeared behind a nearby tree line. No sound could be detected. Mrs Watson, amazed at the extraordinary sight, explained that light shone out from the outer edge, as if coming from windows. The mystery objects appeared to be solid and metallic, and appeared to be spinning rapidly. Two objects led the formation with the third trailing. They were fairly close together.

'The sky was patchy and overcast, but quite bright. The three witnesses recall disbelieving a near similar description, also made in daylight, by another family member and neighbours from the same location a few years ago.'

Mangere Bridge 28th June 1976

Only four days later, just after 11am., Leon Round was working at the carpentry bench in his back garden. He noticed something in the sky was glinting in the sun's rays. He looked up, and could see an object in the southwest, one-and-a-half miles distant, at an elevation of about thirty degrees.

As it came closer, he grabbed his camera, and took a series of six photographs, which clearly showed a disc-type, grey, domed object. The strange craft, which was at least thirty feet in diameter, came within five hundred yards of his home, briefly hovering a couple of times, whilst swaying from side to side and moving up and down in a rhythmic motion. Within seconds, it resumed its flight, and sped off into the distance.

Auckland 1st October 1976

Mrs Thompson of Kaukapakapa, inland from Kaipara Harbour, and northwest of Auckland, was mystified when, at 11pm., she saw an object, 'like a big orange light', which gradually changed to blue, cross the night sky. It was travelling in a southerly direction, and she later commented to researcher Rex Gilroy; *"I later learnt that a good many other people also saw the object that night. Someone must have phoned the Air Force, because a jet fighter flew over the area not long afterwards. Otherwise, the whole matter was 'hushed up' in the media by the military".*

Rex also wrote; *'Several light aircraft were in the Hellensville area one day in September 1978, when a large, silvery, disc-shaped craft flew high over the area. The pilots all reported seeing it, and there were other reports of the same craft as it shot across the sky over Auckland at terrific speed out to sea. Once again, a big cover-up followed.'*

Nelson 13th December 1976

Mr. Gatchell was standing outside with his friend in the Tahuna area, admiring the clear sky, when they spotted a fast moving light, which was coming closer. After about ten seconds, they could distinguish a typical round saucer-type shape, with a red, steady light on top, and small, circular red, green and white coloured lights, which appeared to be rotating in a clockwise direction around the edge. They heard a 'deep power sound', as it passed by at an altitude of about 1,000ft. The two men calculated that since it covered a distance of thirty miles in about thirty seconds, its speed must have equated to about 3,600 mph.

Blenheim 2nd April 1977

Between 11.40pm and 11.45pm, Mrs. Dell could hear a strange noise, as if someone was throwing stones on their roof. She opened the bedroom window, and looked out to see if she could spot the culprits, but no-one was there.

As she stared into the clear night sky, she could see a bright, yellow light in the vicinity of the moon. It appeared to be getting larger, as if moving towards her, so she called out to her daughter, Theresis, to come and watch.

It was travelling from west to east, and when it stopped, they could see a saucer-type craft, revolving in a clockwise direction. It had eight or ten square windows, along the lower part, which suddenly lit up with a bright white glow. The upper portion, or domed area, also had three or four white lights or portholes, but the one on the right had what appeared to be an 'electric blue glowing light'.

The craft did not illuminate the ground below, and when mother and daughter raced to another part of the house, to get a better view, they could no longer locate its position in the sky.

Karangahake 7th June 1977

Barry McLeod, a carpenter with the County Council, was driving home from Waikino at about 8.15pm, when he was startled to see the whole road ahead brilliantly illuminated; *'above and in front of me, in the top of my windscreen, a large object was travelling a little faster than me, and emitting this brilliant light. I estimated it to be thirty to thirty-five feet across, (much wider than the road), about forty feet above the road, and maybe fifty yards ahead. I immediately stopped the car at the side of the road, and got out.'*

His description resembled the top of a mushroom, (without the stalk), with two pale lighted windows, and a dull red light coming from underneath. At this stage it was travelling away from him at about 60mph, and rising at an angle of twenty-five to thirty degrees as it went. He admitted being a bit scared, and shaken up by the experience.

Great Barrier Island 1977

On 31st July, the *'Sunday News'* published an article suggesting that UFOs may have an underwater base off Great Barrier Island. After noting the large number of saucer sightings around the Firth of Thames and the Coromandel Peninsula, they went on to say; *'One man who regularly fishes in the area about five miles to the east of Great Barrier told the 'Sunday News' this week; "I have seen an object come out of the sea and disappear into the sky on two occasions now. It scared the hell out of me, and I didn't tell anyone at the time, in case they reckoned I was a bit nuts".....The fisherman described a 'glowing, silver disc', that 'jumped from the sea and sped off into the sky at incredible speed.'*

'.....About five years ago a Tairus motel owner and friend were fishing six miles off Great Barrier when they saw and photographed a 'sea saucer'. It had emerged quickly from the sea near them, and rapidly become airborne. That part of the ocean was described as being extremely deep.

Kawerau 3rd August 1977

It was about 4am on Wednesday morning when Mrs. Anne Curtin, who lived four kilometres north of Kawerau, and one mile from the airstrip, saw a bright spinning object in the sky. It was saucer-shaped, and flashing red and blue lights. Anne looked out of the window, and determined that whatever it was, it was on the other side of the road and railway lines, and twenty-five to thirty metres above a paddock, about 150 metres away from the house.

She called out to her sister, Joy Morrison, who rushed in and also gaped in astonishment; "I could see a saucer-shaped object from the window", she said. "It tilted for a moment, and I could see the bottom part spinning very quickly, giving off flashes of red and orange light. There was a white light on top, and the other lights were rotating downwards."

It started slowly moving away to the north, parallel with the railway line, so along with Joy's daughter, they rushed outside. The strange craft made a shallow climb as it moved off, and rose higher, about a kilometre away, before hovering for about four minutes. By this time, they had been joined by Joy's husband, and all four witnesses watched as the object suddenly 'took off' towards the east – at great speed – climbing in a straight line until it passed out of sight.

North Auckland 30th January 1978

The Dickesons, in their *'Xenolog'* publication, reported on the following event. *'For years strange lights have been noted in the area, out to sea, and slightly south of Great Barrier Island.*

'Mystery objects have been reported diving from the skies into the waters of the triangular-shaped area. One theory was that they were space-ships re-entering an underwater base. A new theory is the area may be a rendezvous for space-ships needing repair, refuelling or collecting fresh crews or passengers. A sighting that supports this theory was made recently by Beach Haven woman, Lee Arnerich.

'Mrs. Arnerich was on holiday at her family's Martins Bay bach, (holiday house), just north of Auckland. Early one morning she awoke to an unusual 'buzzing' noise, which seemed to fill the bach. She looked outside, and thus began one of the most unusual spacecraft sightings ever reported in New Zealand. Mrs Arnerich saw what appeared to be a link-up between a mother ship and two smaller craft for a repair job.

'For more than an hour, she watched in amazement as three men appeared to climb ladders between the ships – and beam coloured lights at various parts of them. The night was clear, and the thirty feet high, rectangular objects were about one hundred feet up in the sky.

'During the sightings, Mrs. Arnerich's dog became extremely frightened, and at one stage, because of the dog's fear, she had to abandon an attempt to get nearer to the objects. She later said that the lights were silver, gold and orange colour.

'As the lights flashed between the objects, she thought she saw a ladder hanging down mid-section. Part of the big ship was in semi-darkness, and Mrs. Arnerich saw a man in a wetsuit-like garment climb the ladder, and join two

others. The spacecraft manoeuvred gently around each other, and flashed beams between themselves during the hour she watched them.

'Finally, their repairs finished, they headed out southwards towards Tiritiri Island, and disappeared over Rangitoto Island.

Picton/Blenheim 6th February 1978

Murray Miller, a young CBer, and member of the local Search and Rescue organisation, was driving home from Picton to Blenheim one night. Whilst traversing a lonely stretch of swamp road, between Koromiko and Tua Marina, a UFO 'appeared from nowhere', and floated in front of his car.

He described it as being about fifteen feet in diameter, and at an altitude of between three to four hundred feet. He could see its clear-cut edges, and it was perfectly round, white and as bright as the sun in daylight. When he slowed down, or sped up, the object did the same, always keeping just ahead of him. Just before he entered the built-up area of Tua Marina, the UFO quickly sped off and disappeared from sight.

Murray put his foot on the accelerator, and sped home to Blenheim, only getting out of his car when he had ensured the strange craft was no longer in sight.

Hamilton, March 1978

John had been having dinner at his friend's house, and afterwards Murray drove him home. Brian, Murray's eight-year-old son, had insisted on coming, and was seated in the back of the car.

"It was Brian who drew our attention to a large yellow pulsating light hovering, at treetop level, over some nearby houses. At first it was a little obscured, and as we got closer we could see it was an elliptical shape, very large, like a "hotdog-on-end." While it was pulsating, it did not illuminate the surrounding area.

"After a short time it moved silently away to the northwest. One aspect of this incident had me intrigued. Over dinner, Brian had asked me if I believed in UFOs, and I told him about something I had seen in Noumea in 1967. A couple of hours later we sight one! Coincidence, or what?"

Rapaura May 1978

A Blenheim mother and daughter were driving along Rapaura Road at 7.30pm one night. (Exact date unknown). When they spotted an unusual object in the sky, the mother insisted, against her daughter's wishes, on stopping the car to get a better view.

The craft, which was 'cruising' from north to south, 'had a very shiny, silvery appearance, and glowed all over the top like a beautiful, hazy halo'. It was the size and shape of a 'full moon', and was revolving. Three flashing lights, red, green and yellow, appeared and disappeared as the object was moving and rotating. When it stopped, and hovered, the object stopped spinning, and the two women could see its shape, which was that of a domed disc, with the three flashing lights on the bottom.

By this time, the daughter, who was quite scared, wanted to start the car and leave, but her mother, who was fascinated, refused, and they sat and watched the hovering craft for ten minutes until it gently glided away and disappeared over the Whither Hills, which are approximately three miles south of the centre of Blenheim city.

The mother said that whilst her daughter displayed fear and panic, she had felt a sense of awe and fascination, and a feeling of loss when the object went away.

Algies Bay Late May 1978

A twenty-seven year old woman, along with three seventeen year old girls, who were staying at her flat, watched for several minutes as a strange craft hovered above the Bay, before passing directly over them. It was described as being flat underneath, and dome-shaped on top. It had red and green lights, flashing alternatively.

The older woman also mentioned that five years earlier, her sister was on an outing to Martin's Bay, with a teacher and twenty-five other kids. Everyone was enjoying a barbeque on the beach, when a similar type UFO appeared overhead, terrifying most of the children.

Mosgiel October 1978

Lee Blackmore wrote the following to *'MUFON's'* George Filer; *'My first unexplained sighting happened in a small town on South Island called Mosgiel, in 1978, when I was fourteen years old. It was about 8.15pm, sometime in October, and very warm. I was making my mother a cup of tea.*

'At first I heard a rumbling sound, similar to thunder, and as the rumbling got closer, the windows started to shake. The lights in the house were flickering on and off, and the TV reception was going haywire. I looked up at the sky above the trees, which were bent over, as if pulled to the ground by their tops.

'A huge shadow was coming over the house, and the thunder-like sound had changed to a low whoop-whoop. As the shadow grew larger and larger you could see faint greyish coloured lights. The shadow was now a definite shape, outlined by the grey lights. A huge disc was only about thirty metres above the house, (probably higher, but it sure was close and very large). It filled up the sky. The trees were still doing their dance, swinging back and forth like crazy.

'As the disc passed over the house, three very bright lights were visible from the back: one red, one green and one yellow, octagon in shape and looking like honeycomb. The sound seemed overwhelmingly loud, but in reality it wasn't. The sound felt like it was in my head, not in the room. Very disorientating. The disc then sped off south at an alarming rate, towards Dunedin, over Saddle Hill.

'The lights in the house had stopped flickering, and the trees were calm again. I am not sure at what point the sound stopped. Overall, this experience only took two minutes. Over the next week, there were reports in the paper, and on the radio, as far south as Tairei Mouth, (60km away).

Rotorua 5th January 1979

At 5am, Mrs West was awakened by a bright light shining into the room, through her bedroom window. She looked out to see a strange object, hovering about twenty feet off the ground. It was approximately fifty yards away, and was shaped like an inverted top, with a clear section on top, and a long, narrow window about halfway down. There was a yellow glow around the periphery, and a red glow inside. The bottom part seemed to be stationary, whilst the top half was rotating.

It was silently hovering and pulsating above some wavering trees, before moving off after about sixty seconds. She mentioned noticing a strange smell, and the cats in her room seemed very frightened, with their fur 'standing on end'.

Auckland 22nd January 1979

The captain and crew of the thirty metre launch *'Ngorama',* spent three anxious hours whilst off the Coramandel Coast. They had left Tauranga at 1.30am, and after passing Mayor Island at about 3.15am, noticed two sets of lights, which they first thought were planes. When they realised that they weren't moving, Captain Sowerby asked deck hand Mr Kerslake, to take a look through the binoculars.

He saw that one of the objects resembled a 'perfect disc', like a saucer on its side. It had a green and white light around the edge, and a red glow in the middle. The objects suddenly disappeared, and the men thought they had been 'seeing things' until after a couple of minutes they came back. The strange craft continued to disappear and reappear as the launch continued towards Auckland.

Captain Sowerby woke his son, who was the Assistant Captain, and together they watched as the objects seemed to keep pace with them along the coast. One, which came within 400 metres of the launch, was at least the size of their own boat, but was too bright to discern any details. Shortly after, more of the objects appeared, and the men counted as many as fourteen at one time. They were switching their lights on and off, as if keeping in contact with each other.

After three hours, and sixty kilometres of being paced, the Captain and crew were relieved when, just before daybreak, they lost sight of their unusual companions.

Otaio 14th May 1979

At about 3.45pm, when Mr Bird, along with his wife and two children, was driving from Waimata to Timaru, he looked out over the sea and saw a strange object, hovering about a mile away, over the water.

He stopped the car, and got out. At first sight, the unusual craft looked like an upside down pudding plate. Suddenly, it took off to the north, covering about a mile in two seconds, before stopping again. It turned, and came back, slowly and steadily, below the rain clouds. He could see that it was 'pretty big', a dull aluminium colour, with no visible lights. After the family had been watching for about five minutes, the object suddenly shot up into the clouds, and disappeared from view.

Whakatane 14th July 1979

The Dickeson's publication, '*Xenolog*', reported on Mrs. Rose Barnfield and her eleven-year-old daughter, Debbie, who, at 9.15pm, were returning home from Whakatane to Ohape. It was hilly country, and after turning a corner, about forty feet along, she looked up and exclaimed; "My God, Debbie, look at that!"

She said; "I didn't get a good look at it, because I was driving, but it was huge. I was so frightened, I just put my foot down and took off. I travelled another fifty yards before turning off down Alexander Ave." She headed home, even though Debbie was keen to go back and have another look.

The object had been hovering silently, about forty feet above the road. They described it as being about thirty feet in diameter, silver and spherical, with square windows, projecting strong red-orange lights in the lower portion.

Motunau 27th October 1979

June and Norman Neilson, at Motunau, 98kms north of Christchurch, had recently bought a new crayfish fishing boat, of which they were very proud. On 27th October, asked their friend Lou Blackburn, to take a photograph of it, at sunrise, as it was going out of the tidal river mouth.

The film was processed in December, and it was only later, when another friend was looking at the photos through a slide viewer, that, in the sky, an unusual formation of dazzling blue-white lights was noticed. Eventually, Fred and Phyllis Dickeson, photographic experts in their own right, were able to examine the negatives, which they pronounced to be genuine.

They were intrigued with the sparkling diamond-like clearness of the blue-white light which was radiating from the object. They examined the enlargements, and said that there appeared to be eight lights on top of the apparently oval-shaped object, with six underneath, and perhaps five more in-between. Each light seemed to split into two sources, not just one as they first thought. The top row, and all the others, except for the two lower left lights, were blue-white in colour. The two lower left lights appeared to have a cream tinge about them, and between the two rows of lights on the extreme right, there appeared to be a large purplish hazy spot.

This brings to mind a similar photograph taken on super-8 film, twelve years earlier, in May or June 1967, by Ellis Matthews, in Alberton South Australia. Certified by the experts as being genuine, it also depicted an oval type craft, enveloped in a vivid panorama of blue light, with a possible concentric ring around its circumference.

CHAPTER SEVEN

THE GISBORNE FLAP

The Gisborne Flap, 1977–1978

At the time, Gisborne, which had a population of well over 20,000, was known for its fish, vegetables and wine making. A review of the local library indicated that very few, if any, of the population had access to, or read books on UFOs. In 1977, there was a sudden spate of reports of inexplicable lights and objects in the sky.

There was a small group of eight enthusiasts in the town, who found themselves suddenly overwhelmed when asked to look into these unusual events.

My colleague Bryan Dickeson, was living in Wellington at the time, close to ground zero. He was able to visit Hamish McLean of the Gisborne '*APRG'*, several times during this memorable and much-publicised UFO flap which occurred between November 1977 and March 1978. Bryan conducted a very thorough investigation into the entire phenomena.

"When I flew to Gisborne", Bryan said, "I did not expect to find anything quite so startling. I found the local group had carefully recorded as much detail of the different events as it could, and had taken steps to authenticate the material it had collected."

Hamish himself witnessed an unidentified craft at 10.20 a.m. on 29th November, 1977. He had received a call from a farmer in the Waimata Valley, sixteen kilometres from Gisborne: a flying saucer had landed in a nearby paddock. Hamish immediately set out to see for himself. At first he saw nothing, but as he drove around a bend in the valley, he saw the flying saucer.

He described it as being shaped like a large bowler hat; a fluorescent pink-red dome with a boomerang shaped frieze across the middle and five dark grey, rectangular line markings on the surface underneath. The boomerang frieze itself was white with purple characters across it, like foreign-written symbols. There was a deep bright metallic blue rim below the dome. Underneath the rim were four dull grey square pads or feet, and four hazy green cylinders of light, with a slightly denser green light spiralling within. Hamish watched the stationary object for about three minutes. Suddenly a bright beam of blue light shot out of a small square aperture on its lower left side. It focussed on a dead tree, some fifteen metres away, which lit up like a Christmas tree. The beam lasted about seven seconds, during which time each tree branch radiated fluorescent-coloured light of different hues. Sheep in the paddock near the tree, immediately started bleating and ran away down the hill, where they milled about in small groups. (Later examination of the tree showed no apparent damage, even the resident spiders seemed unaffected.)

McLean Object
Gisborne N.Z. 29 Nov. 1977

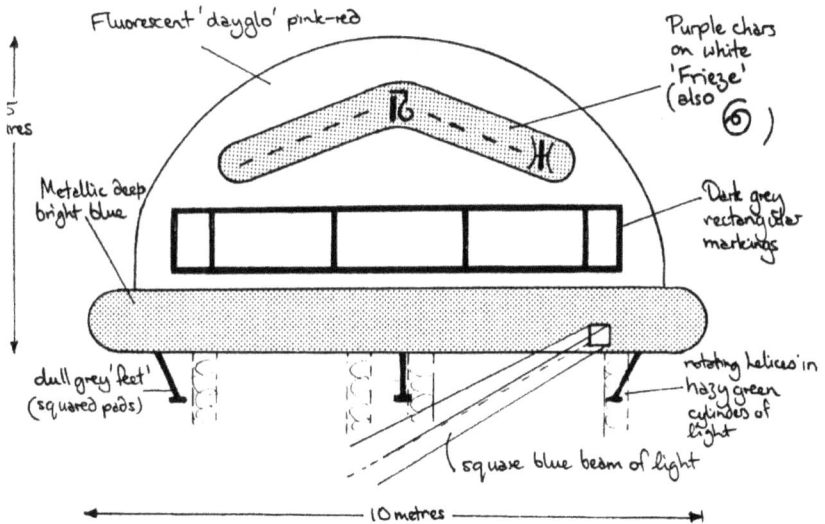

When Hamish had stopped the car and got out, the object was 150 metres to his left, and 100 metres above the road, slightly above a hill. The craft now moved fifteen metres to the right, hovered for two minutes, then swept back behind the hillside. It re-emerged back to its original place above the hillside where Hamish first saw it. It hovered there for a few minutes, so Hamish raced to the nearest farmhouse to ring another researcher.

Hamish was working part-time as a cadet reporter for the local newspaper. There had been many bogus calls, and when this witness called him, he had not expected to see anything. Now he wanted corroboration, and drove back to town to fetch a colleague. Unfortunately, by the time they returned, the object was nowhere to be seen.

The next week more unusual events were reported, which were difficult for Bryan and Hamish to confirm. However the witnesses were country people, not connected, and seemed genuine. Some of the details they gave corroborated previously undisclosed data.

9th December 1977
A small bright red light was seen at 7.30 p.m., and later at 10.40 p.m., a bright, fast-moving red object, shaped like an "upside-down frying pan", was hovering behind a hill where it had joined a similar blue object. For several minutes they hovered side by side, moved back and forth, and then took off up into the valley at high speed.

During January and February many reports of unidentified lights and craft intrigued the local media and researchers. It was referred to as the 'Gisborne Flap', with most sightings centred on the Waimata Valley. (The valley itself has a significant, though overlooked history. During the Maori Land Wars of the 19th century, European farmer-settlers were massacred there. Most Maori still consider it to be a sad and haunted place.)

Many Gisborne people hoped to see one of these strange objects for themselves. It was a great opportunity to take a picnic, or midnight snack, and go out to the valley on a warm summer night.

Waimata Valley 2nd December 1977

Perhaps the most memorable sequence of events occurred when a Waimata Valley farmer was woken, at about 3am., by his dogs barking. He raced out the back door with his rifle, and was stunned to see a landed flying saucer to his right.

His description was similar to the bowler hat craft Hamish had seen the previous week. It was thirty to forty feet across, with a metallic outer shell, which glowed bright blue, and had an unusual boomerang shape drawing on the outside.

He also saw open rectangular doors, with an intensely bright red interior. To the left of the object he saw two humanoid figures, about four foot, eight inches tall, wearing close-fitting metallic silver overalls, cuffed at the bottom over red, glowing boots. They had white opaque helmets, extended across their shoulders, and their hands were covered with flared gauntlets extending halfway up their forearms.

Location 1:

Gisborne, NZ

Latitude 38°40' South
Longitude 178°01' East

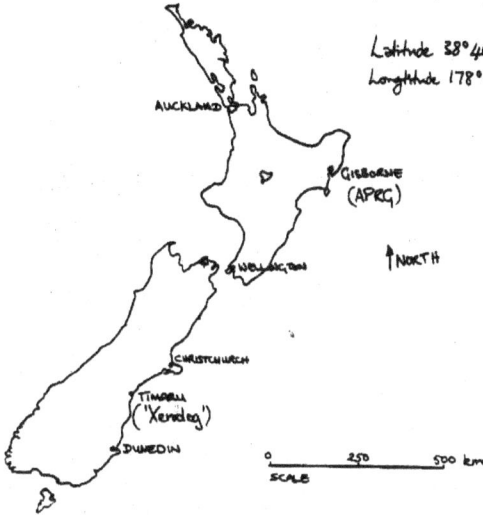

AUCKLAND

GISBORNE
(APRG)

↑NORTH

WELLINGTON

CHRISTCHURCH

TIMARU
('Xendeg')

DUNEDIN

0   250   500 km
SCALE

Between them they were carrying the limp, upside-down body of one of his sheep dogs. The farmer shot at the beings, winging one, who dropped the dog and ran into nearby bushes. The second being ran for the craft, which took off vertically, at great speed, after the doors closed behind him. The dog got up, rather groggy and started jumping around and barking.

Investigators received an unconfirmed report that later in the morning of 2nd December, a local, who went up the valley every day, found the farmer, whose dog had nearly been abducted, sitting in a chair, with a shotgun on his lap, and still in a very dazed condition.

There was an interesting turn of events: Six days later, at 7 p.m. on 8th December, a man driving down the Waimata Valley Road saw a "small man" trying to flag him down on the left-hand side of the road. Initially he slowed down, but had second thoughts and sped up and headed to town.

He described the hitchhiker as being four feet, nine inches tall, wearing a silver suit and red boots. He was not wearing a helmet, and was jumping up and down and frantically waving. Was this the being left behind after the failed dog-napping attempt?

Although this is speculation on my part, I wonder if several sightings, in the Waimata Valley, after 2nd December were the visitors searching for their missing comrade?

There were a couple of reports from the Waimata Valley, on the 3rd December - one of a yellowish light, and another of a craft, thirty metres across, and similar to what was seen by Hamish McLean, which came within 150 metres of the witness.

Location 2:

Waimata Valley, Gisborne N.Z.

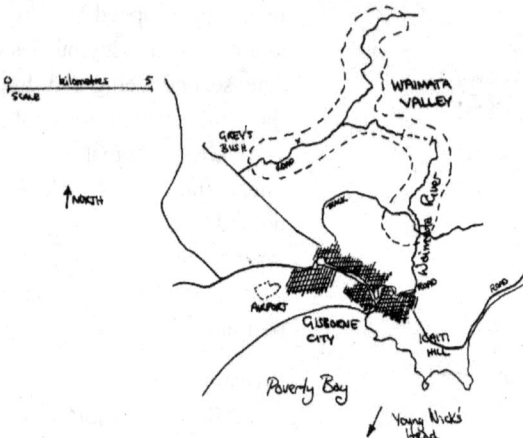

One researcher was turning his car round, while a colleague waited at the roadside. A huge green object, about one hundred feet across, came from behind a hill, just above the road, to the left and about thirty-five metres in front of him. It only hovered for a few seconds before moving back behind the hill.

As the reports came flooding in, Bryan Dickeson decided to join the local researchers, and further investigate the entire scenario. He wrote; *'Gisborne is geographically separate from most of New Zealand, and yet very accessible by sea and road. It has a population of about 33,000, and although its original role as the provincial port is now in decline, it remains the trading centre of a rich pastoral and agricultural district.*

'New Zealand has a fairly uniform culture, and a narrow social and wealth range. Gisborne provides a good cross-section sample of the 'middle class' population of New Zealand.... The incidents were highly localised around the Gisborne area itself, and particularly some five kilometres north of the city in the vicinity of the Waimata Valley.'

There had been multiple reports of unidentified lights in the sky, plus sightings of more detailed craft, close up. There appeared to be two surges of reports, one before Christmas 1977, followed by another in the New Year. Bryan noted; *'A complex series of more than one hundred UFO events was recorded in considerable detail between late 1977 and early 1978....The 1977 reports provide some of the most detailed UFO data ever to come out of New Zealand between 1952 and 1984. Furthermore, the latter Gisborne reports show signs of distortion in the data, which may be directly attributable to the effect of unprecedented publicity in the local media. These records require further assessment.'*

Gisborne June 1976

There had been a few earlier sightings in the area. One Sunday, at 2.30 p.m., a retired couple was driving northwest along the highway towards Frasertown. There was far less traffic than normal, for such a clear, sunny day.

Mrs.A was driving, and about 250 metres directly in front of the car, she saw an object which swooped down just above their vehicle. It quickly sped directly towards the car, and suddenly stopped about 100 metres ahead, on the right hand side of the road. Mrs. A slowed the car to a halt, hesitant to go closer.

It was bright silver, twenty to thirty metres across, and looked like "an inverted dinner plate, with a cupola dome on top." There were no obvious markings, except a line of small, evenly spaced dark apertures on the side. Neither she nor her husband noticed any noise or smell.

For five or six minutes the craft proceeded to tumble, roll and speed around in a tight circle, before speeding off to the hills in the northeast.

Whangara Valley 6th June 1977

One of the first reports received in this current 'flap', had come from north of Gisborne at about 5.30pm, when three witnesses saw a disc shaped object – red, orange and green – with a glowing white band 'around its outside'. It was only 400m away, and fifteen metres above the tree-line. It hovered soundlessly for thirty minutes, before heading slowly towards Gisborne.

Waimata Valley Early November 1977

During this 'flap', many of the reports came from an area a few miles inland, known as the Waimata Valley, which is quite narrow, and twenty miles long with steep sides. One of the initial reports, received in early November, came from a Maori farmer's wife. At the far end of the valley, she and her husband had seen what appeared to be a 'mother ship' and several discs.

At 9.15pm, on 29th November, a witness reported seeing a white point source exiting the valley, and an hour-and-three-quarters later, a group of five people saw a red and blue spherical object in the region. It was about the size of the moon, and swooped within 350 metres above them, before moving away at a very fast rate.

Waimata Valley December 1977

However, on 6th December, the strange craft were a little more active. The farmer from the 'dog-napping' event rang to say that three objects, similar to the ones he had previously reported, were hovering near his house. When investigators went out they had already gone,

Gisborne resident, Mr. Cooper, was travelling into the valley at 1.15am, when he rounded a corner to be confronted by a large disc-shaped object, one to two hundred feet above the road. It was bright red, and flickering, and quickly moved behind a hill.

At 11.45 a.m. a man, travelling along the road south of Gisborne, reported being paced for half a mile, by a bright object, about 100 metres away. His dog, in the back seat, growled, and raised the hackles on the back of his neck, during the incident. The craft was described as being larger than a 50c piece, with clearly defined edges.

At 6.40 p.m. five people in a car were paced, for two km, by a spherical object, also similar to the one seen by Hamish Mclean. They were travelling northwest from Gisborne, towards Ormond. It was about 125 metres away and only six metres above the ground. It sped up until 375 metres ahead, and started zig-zagging across the road, causing an oncoming vehicle to nearly run off the road. (A truck driver, travelling some distance behind, also witnessed this event. Looking rather stunned, he pulled up, and after a few words, drove away.)

An hour later at 7.30 p.m. three women, driving along the coast road, had a similar experience, when an object followed them for about a mile, sixty metres away from their car. When they stopped, to get a better look, the strange craft veered off into the hills towards the Waimata Valley. They described the metallic object as being 'as big as a dinner plate', with a large cupola top over the base.

In fact, all the witnesses that day described a bowler-hat shaped craft. Two days later, and again on 9th December, further witnesses saw a similar object heading, at high speed, in the direction of the Valley.

One witness, from 8th December, told of how the object, which she sighted at 10.40pm, resembled an 'upside-down' frying pan, was joined by a similar 'blue' coloured object, and after hovering together for a few minutes, they appeared to move back and forth before taking off, at high speed, into the Waimata Valley. Other reports of strange craft were also reported on the 13th and 20th of the month.

1978

In early January, especially the 19th, multiple witnesses reported unusual lights in the sky, especially over the Waimata Valley. A more detailed report was received on 15th January, when for forty-five minutes, six people watched a large craft, estimated to be 750ft in diameter, diving up and down, backwards and forwards, over Grays Bush Hill, at the entrance to the Waimata Valley.

On 2nd February, a group of young people, parked on a road in the valley, heard a continuous humming noise approaching. At first, they thought it was another car, but then a huge, dark shadowy shape, giving off orange 'spotlights', passed overhead. They calculated it as being about twice the size of the car, travelling twenty to thirty miles per hour, and about ten to eleven feet above the ground. Their car shook as the object passed over, and the humming sound grew fainter as the object moved away. The whole event lasted about twenty to thirty seconds.

At 9.45pm, on 3rd February, a Tatapouri couple watched for five minutes as a large, silver, oval object, about the size of a helicopter, hovered over the Valley. As it moved round and behind the hills, it glistened, and radiated a glow which lit up a large area.

The previous evening, a young couple, living in an isolated area outside Warkworth, had seen strange lights in the sky on previous nights. On this occasion, the husband stood at the back door, and flashed his torch in their direction. The light suddenly descended, and appeared to land in a paddock fifty metres away.

It was silver and round – a glowing saucer-shape – with blinking lights. A door opened, and the witness saw a tall person standing in the doorway. The husband waved to the 'man', who apparently waved back before the door closed, and the craft rose to about fifteen metres before 'taking off'.

Gisborne 11th February 1978

This particular summer Saturday brought forth more reports than usual. The Dickesons' *'Xenolog'* publication quoted from the *'Gisborne Herald'* – *'Photo taken of star-like object as it rose in the air from behind trees, casting brilliant green, red and orange lights – three exposures were taken.*

'Fourteen sightings reported this week. Two men in Waimata Valley looked back towards Gisborne city. They witnessed a large, oblong object, about the size of a bus, spinning along Gray's Bush Hill, and giving off red and white lights.

'Two people in the Elgin area, west of Gisborne, were tying up their dog, when they heard a low humming noise from willow trees on their property. A large thirty foot disc-shaped object, giving off a yellow light, was hovering sixty feet above the ground. – At 10.30pm, ten witnesses on Gray's Bush Hill, who were looking into the Waimata Valley, noticed four blue lights in the sky, with a white light jumping from one to another.' There were other witnesses in the area who also reported the same phenomena. At the same time, a party of six, on the top of Gray's Bush Hill, saw lights and beams in the sky, and twenty minutes later, two objects flew overhead.

At 1am, the next morning, fisherman Leo Penno, was startled when a UFO, 'as big as a house', hovered for about three minutes, two hundred feet over the 'outer reef'. It climbed to about 260ft, and at some 1,2000ft away, the surface of the UFO broke out into a constant flow of varied coloured lights for nearly thirty seconds. Leo estimated the craft as being about forty feet in diameter.

It then moved inland, just passing over a coastal hill, and as it went, a reddish/blue or purplish light flashed on and off. He said the event 'scared the hell' out of him, and he rowed back to shore as fast as possible.

2nd March 1978

Just before 6am, a middle-aged man, on his way to work, saw a red-orange 'sausage-shaped' object, with a dome on top, speeding across the sky towards Waimata Valley. Sometime later, a man driving through Makaraka stopped his car to view a similar object, which he reported as being twice the size of a house.

5th March 1978

A factory worker, having finished the late shift, was driving to a relative's house when his car was filled with an orange glow. About fifty feet away was the tail end of a huge, square-shaped floating object, easily the size of a three storey building, and exceptionally long. After passing it, he looked back to see it had gained height and was speeding off towards the Waimata Valley.

Waihi 9th March 1978

Several members of a family raced outside when one of them saw a silver, elliptical disc, lit up around the edges, spinning low in the sky. It soon quickly rose and sped off over the hills.

12th March 1978

The *'Gisborne Herald'* detailed a report from 12th March, when a mill worker at Kawerau was driving back to Gisborne, early in the morning. A brilliant orange light suddenly lit up the interior of his car. When he looked out the window, he got 'the shock of his life!' About fifty feet away was a large oval object, with multiple small lights along the side, floating alongside his car. As he drove along the road, he closely scrutinised the object, which he estimated to be the size of a five storey building.

He watched as it silently rose three to four hundred feet into the sky, and said he had never seen anything like that before – and never wanted to see it again!

Four days later, at 5.40am on 16th March, a woman looked out of her window to see an oval object, about 1,000ft away, which was moving across Poverty Bay Flats. She raced back to her bedroom and grabbed her binoculars. She said the object, which looked solid, was bright red, with silver lines down the side, which gave the appearance of coloured windows.

As it was moved past her house, in a westerly direction, towards the Waimata Valley, she first heard a humming sound, then a pulsating, heavy drumming noise, 'nothing like an aeroplane makes'.

There were multiple accounts of lights in the sky during February and early March, by which time the reports seemed to peter out.

Between Long Bush and Pirihaua 22nd August 1978

There was, however, still the odd interesting report. Two young lads, Phillip Baker and his cousin, Howard Baker, were holidaying in a hut, 750ft. above sea level, on a sheep station where Howard's father worked.

At about 9.15pm., during a break in what had been rainy weather, the boys ventured out onto the hilltop. Suddenly, they noticed a strange light, coming up the valley, from the direction of the sea. It was travelling quickly towards them, and as it came nearer, they could see, down below, a strange craft which resembled a 'bowler hat'. It had a light glow on top, was red in the middle, blue underneath, and had yellow and white beams shining down onto the valley below.

When, what was obviously a solid object, came within fifty feet of them, the lads dived for cover under nearby scrub. They watched as it passed very low over their hut, and gauged it to have a diameter of eighty to one hundred feet. As soon as it moved off behind a hill, they rushed back to the hut. Mr. Baker said that his son and his friend had burst through the door in a very agitated state.

Gisborne "close encounters"

2nd February 1978
Three friends, Bronwyn Pauls, Ida Bishop and Sally Jones, (pseudonyms), made occasional overnight trips to the valley, for stargazing and gossip as a break from shift-work and family responsibilities. Hubby would mind the kids while they had a giggle and reminisced on days gone by. At 5.10 a.m. while parked on the Waimata Valley Road near its junction with Manders Road, their girl talk was interrupted by a continuous buzzing noise:

"At first we thought it was someone driving down the road, but there was no sound of gear change or engine variation. A huge, dark shadowy shape passed very low, about ten or twelve feet above our car, which started to shake. It was twice the size of a car, and emanating orange spotlights. It would have been travelling at about twenty-thirty miles per hour, and we could hear the continuous roar as it proceeded up the valley.

"We had seen a few odd lights a bit earlier, but nothing like this. We were determined to have another night out in the near future, to see what else we could observe."

Two months later, my colleague Bryan Dickeson conducted an in-depth investigation into this and subsequent incidents, and wryly commented that they might have heeded the old adage: "Be careful what you wish for!"

11–12 March 1978
It was nice, mild Saturday evening and Bronwyn, Ida and Sally thought it would be fun to go back to the valley and camp out overnight. Winter was coming and there would be few opportunities left for more 'girls' nights' out.

Bronwyn detailed the events that evening: "We arrived about 10 p.m., parked the car just off the side of the road, out of sight, and walked up a steep hill nearby. We had a great view of the lower Waimata Valley, and could still watch our vehicle parked below. The previous time, inside the car, our view of any object was restricted. This time, if anything turned up, we could see it a lot better. We snuggled into our sleeping bags; I positioned myself between Ida and Sally, it felt a bit safer!"

The UFO "fever" had one unpleasant aspect: groups of youths, a few armed with guns, had sometimes taken to cruising the road at night hoping to get a pot-shot at something. At about 11 p.m. a carload of people came down the road with headlights on full-beam and radio blaring. The women covered anything light-coloured which might attract attention in the dark, and settled down to wait for the hoons to go.

"A little later we heard a distinct noise, like tin cans buckling. This lasted about twenty minutes. We kept chatting for about another thirty minutes, and must have dozed off before midnight. I woke with a start at about 1 am., Ida and Sally were still asleep, but there was someone I could not see entirely, standing over me. I reached out behind and touched a cool, metallic calf length boot. I just turned over, snuggled up to Ida, and went back to sleep!

"The next thing I remember is kicking Sally with my foot and whispering; "Did you see that? Let's get out of here, it's cold." There was nothing in sight, but somehow we were all starting to panic. It was now 4 a.m. Sunday morning. We grabbed our sleeping bags, rushed down the hill to the car and headed home."

The women were all convinced that "something had happened", but couldn't remember what. They obviously had a total blank for the time period from just after 1 a.m. to 4 a.m. They now felt strangely attracted to that part of the valley and had returned to the spot several times since. Other people who had accompanied them on some of these trips, had also seen luminous objects.

The three women felt uneasy about the two lost hours, and wanted to know if anything odd had happened. However, only the nurse, Bronwyn, was prepared to undergo hypnotherapy:

After they had fallen asleep, Bronwyn recalled waking up on the hillside, shielding her eyes from a bright white light shining down from above. A large disc-shaped object was hovering directly out from where they lay, above the trees just beyond their car. It was hard-edged, with a dome on top. It was a bright white colour, and had yellow lights on the dome and underneath. She also recalled there were a few small red lights.

"It moved closer, and Sally and I were drawn up off the ground and along the bright white light beam towards the craft. The beam held us firmly, but didn't appear to be solid. We could see Ida below, still asleep in her sleeping bag. Sally was struggling and I called out to her: "It's not meant to happen like this!"

Bronwyn's next memory was of being inside a small round room. "I don't know how we got in there. I was lying on a raised horizontal slab of white material, and Sally was on another. There was a panel of coloured lights, and the whole room was a milky white colour. I could see doors, with round lintels, and a faceted column of some sort.

"Sally was looking over at me. There was a male being, average height and fairish appearance dressed in an off-white coverall or uniform, with white boots. (Not *metallic* as she had first thought.) He was talking to me, but his lips weren't moving; it was a long and fairly pleasant conversation.

Bronwyn said he had told her not to divulge what he had told her, and she became extremely angry when the hypnotherapist tried to press her for details.

I have all the initial hypnotherapist's extensive notes from the original session, however, whilst they are much more extensive and detailed, they are marked 'confidential' and I must respect this.

One aspect, I feel a may reveal, is a further description a being who showed her around the craft, where she saw other crew members and equipment. He also explained various reasons for their visits, where they were from, and why they had come here. She explained; "*He had slanted eyes, like the Japanese, fair hair, roundish face, but I did notice that his arms were shorter than normal. He had deep red eyes, brownish cheeks, hair shoulder length, slim build, and was wearing a shiny, one piece, gold suit that came down to his brown boots. He had gold gloves joined on to his suit, and boots also, so the whole garment was one piece.*

When asked if she could remember anything else, Bronwyn said; *"Only that his collar was high, like the ones on the old rock and roll movies. The top of the collar would come up in front to about his cheek, and in the back, right around his neck, his hair would hang over the outside.'*

There was no indication of any kind of physical examination. (Many years later an implant was found, which another colleague of mine was arranging to have removed and examined.)

Bronwyn then remembered being returned to the hillside: "The same light beam seemed to push us back down until we were back on the ground again. For a few moments it bore down on me like a heavy weight. The craft quickly disappeared, and I came to and kicked Sally: "Are you awake?" – "Of course I'm bloody awake!" It was then we woke Ida and headed for the car."

For the next few days, both Bronwyn and Sally experienced unusual headaches. On the night of 17th or 18th March, Les Green, a family friend, drove the three women, who were trying to make sense of what had happened, back to the valley. They went back to the spot where they had camped the previous night, but then climbed higher up to a fence at the top of the hill.

After a while, they noticed some 'red flashing lights with green rotating around the top' on a hill across the valley. It hovered long enough for Les to take a photograph. Fifteen minutes later, it was seen again, moving short distances from left to right. After Les took another snap, they all ran back down the hill, and hopped in the car in order to drive closer.

As they came closer to the strange craft, they realised a bright white light was following them. When they stopped, and jumped out of their vehicle, the white light disappeared, and the object they had been pursuing rose approximately one hundred feet above them.

It was hovering on the side of the hill, and they could clearly see the dome shaped top, with three red pulsating lights, and a green light above. They weren't really able to gauge the actual size of the craft, which disappeared soon after.

At that time the women had very little knowledge of ufology, which prevented any preconceived ideas or fantasy regarding abductions. Further, a hypnotic regression was undertaken soon after the experience, when details were still fresh in their minds. When told of the results both found it rather unbelievable, and declined any further sessions.

The experience did haunt Bronwyn, who started reading a lot more about the subject. In 1989, after moving to Australia, she contacted several other researchers and UFO groups, and agreed to further hypnotherapy with other investigators.

They produced an entirely different report, consisting of a disjointed scenario containing of lots of 'oohs','aahs', and 'go away'-type comments, with few extra meaningful details. This was written up, some eleven years after the encounter, with disparaging remarks regarding the original hypnotherapy. I found Bryan's notes to be excellent, and the procedures definitely in keeping with the highest ethics and protocols. I have no idea whether Bronwyn had further experiences during the next eleven years, or of her later involvement with UFO research or abduction support groups.

Eventually Bronwyn received further assistance from a colleague in Queensland. Two chip implants were located. One, of an unknown metal substance, was removed from her chin, and the other, still in situ, is visible in a foot X-ray.

Next Generation?
In early 2008, some thirty years later, I received a call from Sonja, and realised she was the daughter of one of the three women involved in the 1978 Waimata Valley incident. She was now thirty-four years old, and had lived in Australia since leaving New Zealand with her mother when she was thirteen. She was now in Hawkes Nest, one hour north of Newcastle in New South Wales.

"Despite my mother's experiences, I don't recall seeing anything until the 30th October 2007, when I was camping at Barrington Tops, and saw lots of inexplicable craft in the sky. I haven't seen any actual large traditional UFOs before or since.

"Across the road from where I live, is a large patch of grass about the size of two football fields, leading to a small bay and inlet of water. I used to see lots of white and orange lights, all about twice the size of a planet, on the other side of the water. I know it was silly, but I used to flash my torch, to try and communicate with them. Sometimes there would be a red light over the water – I felt like it was watching me. It wasn't a boat or something conventional as it would levitate up and down in a wobbly fashion. On these occasions I felt some weird sensations, and I would go home with my hair standing on end, and a feeling of heightened senses.

"On 11th January 2008, Melinda, a girlfriend from Brisbane was staying with me. She showed me a light in the sky one night. I thought it was a star, but then it moved. We went back outside after midnight, and took photos of lights zooming in. Just after dawn, on the morning of the 12th January 2008, we could still see something strange, and took more photos of what looked like sparkler trailers, or serpents-gone-wrong.

"That night my sixteen year old daughter, Trudy saw lights in the sky, and took some more pictures. A bit later Melinda thought she saw something else:

"We got the camera, and the three of us went outside. There was a red orb of light over the water. At first we thought it was a boat, but then it split in two, and both objects zig-zagged up and down, and from side to side over a small area.

"We went closer for a better look. The red light was blinking, and we noticed a larger orb of white light, with another white light behind, to the side. It looked like a searchlight, and we could see reflections of a lot of people, both short and tall, and shadows of them scurrying about. We tried to take more photos, but the camera wouldn't work properly, except to give out a big flash, at which time the white light moved to the side of the trees.

"In its full beam we saw very tall, seven to eight-foot beings, with long arms and legs, and oblong almond-shaped heads. They walked, or almost floated, across the grass towards us. I was terrified, and the three of us ran back to the house. After we got through the front door, to the side, in the hallway, I could see an almond-head watching. The baby woke up and was crying; the two children were scared. 'It' stopped moving, stood up watching, and seemed to get taller. Melinda, Trudy and I all felt the same overwhelming weird sensations inside."

When Sonja rang me she was nervous, upset and a little confused. She told me of taking several series of photographs during that period. It seemed they had become abnormally obsessed over a thirty-six hour timeframe. Her report after this became very disjointed and out of sequence.

"My three-year-old, who was inside all the time, now won't sleep in her room. She talks of a nice, beautiful princess, who has a small 'ogre' companion. Trudy had marks on her body – small oblong red welts from her shoulder blade to her waist. These can fade, and reappear in a minute. She spoke of dreaming of a tall, elegant female with dark black almond eyes, which didn't blink, and looked like a camera lens with an oily effect. A few weeks later she told me she had been on a spaceship one night; "They've lost something and are running out of time." She saw pictures of 'wormholes and DNA structures.'

"Melinda is a different matter. She had psychological problems before and used to 'hear' radio waves. She had a strong feeling to come to Hawkes Nest at that time. Now she also dreams of a 'tall, elegant woman', and the doctor says it goes a lot deeper than bi-polar disorder."

Given her mother's experiences with the other two women in New Zealand, I referred the matter to a competent colleague, as I thought these latest events may well be related.

More "missing time" from Gisborne

March 1978
About a month after the three women's experience in the Waimata Valley, there was another disturbing event an hour out of Gisborne, in the Tokomaru Bay area. Suzanne Hansen, the lead New Zealand researcher from *'UFOCUS'*, documented this incident in great detail.

A husband and wife, I shall call them David and Joan, had been shopping and visiting friends in Gisborne. At 10.30 p.m. they started out on their nearly three-hour journey home to East Cape. About an hour later, they reached a high point in the hills and saw a huge area of bright white light, coming up from the paddocks on the valley floor below.

"It was such a shock; we skidded to a halt, and the car stalled. There were a couple of small rises in the landscape which partly obscured our view, but the sides of the valley were bathed in this intense, dense, silvery-white light. It was brighter than daylight, and seemed to permeate every nook and cranny; frightening in its intensity and awesome in its magnitude."

They were both in shock and disbelief, and scared because it was a very remote area, with no telephone or traffic on the road. David tried to reassure Joan with some rational explanation, but Joan wasn't having any of it, and would have preferred to go back to Gisborne rather than drive any further as long as that light was there.

"After a relatively short space of time, I started to feel numb and tingly in my arms and legs," Joan said. "My body suddenly felt tired and heavy and all around me became quiet, distant and vague. I became slightly dizzy and faint, and could hear a deep increasing buzzing sound. I tried to tell David, but don't remember if I did as I couldn't move."

The next thing Joan could recall was just sitting in the car, in darkness. The light had gone, she felt totally drained, and David was almost unresponsive at first. They drove home in silence. (I would note that a loss of conversation after an encounter is frequently reported.)

Over the next few days Joan experienced painful, sensitive hearing, several nosebleeds, and extreme fear at any unexpected noises. David refused to discuss anything about the light or the night trip. That left her feeling very alone with her fears, as she could recall a similar experience in 1975 on a rural road near Hastings.

It took many years, and more unusual experiences before Joan could really come to terms with this and other incidents which had a huge impact on her life and relationship. As in many cases, it was some years before some suppressed memories surfaced from her subconscious.

"Eventually I began to have flashbacks and dream-like recall, culminating in later years in conscious recall of on-board craft experiences, and communications with extraterrestrial entities."

CHAPTER EIGHT

THE 1980s and BEYOND

Near Temuka 12th July 1981

There has been some confusion over the date and details of this sighting, however below is the report written by Fred and Phyllis Dickeson. They immediately interviewed the family on 15th July, following a phone call from Mrs. Thew, two days after the event, on 14th July.

'The UFO sighting occurred four miles east of the Richard Pearce aircraft memorial which was recently erected to commemorate the inventor. As a point of interest, the aircraft pioneer, Richard Pearce, is claimed by some to have flown his craft in 1903, before the American Wright Brothers, on June 11th 1904.

'It was wintery, and had been raining, but the weather was clearing, the sky was 7/10ths cloudy, with a few visible stars peeking through the clear sky patches.

'Mr. and Mrs. Ken Thew, their three daughters, aged nine, six, and three years, were returning home to Temuka, rather later than usual, after visiting friends in the smaller town of Pleasant Point, a distance of eleven miles away.

'They were travelling along the Waitchi-Point back-road to Temuka, had passed the corner on to the Waitchi Main Road, and were half a mile from Moores Road intersection, when they suddenly became aware of a brilliantly lit green-gold-red object coming from the opposite direction, in the east, at about a 20 degree angle.

'The time was 00.50am, Sunday morning 12th July, 1981. Startled, and thinking the lights may have been some kind of reflection on the wet windows, the driver checked by hurriedly winding it down, but the object was still there, and seemed to be heading for the car. The object's size would be about two-thirds the size of the moon at this stage. Then it stopped abruptly, about two or three hundred yards away, changed direction and proceeded to pace the car. It could be easily seen, sometimes behind and through the nearby broken lines of leafless trees. Another four hundred yards further on, they reached the Kakahu

Road corner, and this is where they noticed the UFO coming even lower to the ground.

'Mrs. Thew, who was driving at this stage, became rather scared. Ken wanted to pull over, to get a better view. He even suggested getting out and approaching the object, but his wife began increasing speed from 45mph to 65mph. Her one aim was to get closer to the illuminated area of the Temuka township, and to get away from the open country FAST. The object, in its parallel pacing action, also increased speed to match that of the car.

'Mrs Thew said the extreme brilliance of the light, emanating from the craft, made the car headlights appear very dim. Frantic attempts to brighten them, by manipulating the headlight switch, made no difference.

'After travelling another one-and-a-half miles towards Talbots Road, the UFO came nearer, and was estimated to be only 120 yards away. At this point the car occupants were able to get a very good look, and noted many details. Ken Thew, who is a motor mechanic in Temuka, said; "When the window was opened the object came closer to the car, and much lower, revealing it was something we had never seen before. There was no noise, and at this point it was quite apparent that it was a controllable flying object.'

It was oval, a dark green colour, on top, with the bottom part predominately red. There were square, white windows along the lower half of the craft, and a couple of panels on the side, with possible red type rays, coming from the rear. Later calculations estimated the craft to be somewhere just over thirty feet in diameter and fifteen feet high.

'Both Mrs. Thew, and her eldest daughter were puzzled and intrigued when they observed what was described as a 'fat person, shaped like a 'figure eight' appearing to be outside the craft.

'.... Proceeding further along the road, the object suddenly shot away towards the east. Ken said; "One moment it was close, the next it was in the distance...You didn't see it move between the two points, it was just there!"

'The car reached the outskirts of the Temuka township, but instead of going directly home, the Thews turned south onto the main highway – going towards Timaru – to see if they could get a better view. They could still see the object, as it was changing different colours. They travelled over the Temuka and Opihi *bridges, past the hotel, and stopped at the first crossroads, a distance of about two miles south of Temuka.*

'They continued to watch the craft change colour. It was to the east, towards the sea. It was very low down, but could be seen through the leafless trees in that area, giving them the impression that it was trying to hide. There were quite a number of cars passing their position on the main highway, but as the craft they were watching was very low down, it was understandable that passing motorists would not be aware of it.

'They watched for some time, but a static situation prevailed, so they decided to return home. Arriving at 1.20am, they were surprised to see the craft hovering above them, at about 1,000ft,, when they got out of the car. While they looked at it, the craft headed off towards the east, disappearing behind their home.

'Ken went around the back, and located it hovering, like a helicopter, low in the east, keeping its altitude, but going up, down and sideways. At 2am., Mrs. Thew rang her friends at Pleasant Point, but it was too late for them to also see the strange craft, as Ken called out that it was too late – the object had vanished out of sight.'

Christchurch, 1982

A reader wrote to the Australian *'Ufologist'* magazine, in 2002, about an interesting second-hand report from a 32-year-old man who had lived in Christchurch as a child. At 7 p.m. he and his mother had just returned home when they saw what they thought were several small fires in the hills to the south. They noticed a light moving very quickly towards them from that direction. Eventually it was overhead, where it stopped and silently hovered. Other neighbours were also staring.

It was a huge oval shape, "the size of two football fields" and a sort of a buff colour. They could not see any portholes, just lights coming from the bottom. After about five minutes it moved and took off at high speed. When they went inside and turned on the radio, the announcer said they didn't want any more people calling in about the UFO. They had been instructed to "say nothing."

Lyttelton Harbour 16th November 1991

'UPERS' Christchurch investigated the following case; It was nearly 2am, when the witness was returning to his house after walking a friend home. He noticed

what appeared to be large searchlights coming from a very large object moving slowly above the sea, but below the level of the mountain ridges around Lyttelton Harbour. This would have placed it at an approximate altitude of 150-200 metres.

He ran inside, and his two friends came out and joined him to gaze at the strange craft hovering motionless above the water. They described the soundless object as being metallic, and resembling a 'triangle with a flat, blunt nose'. It had well-defined edges, about twenty-one metres long, and twenty-eight metres at its widest.

There were two distinct rows of lights, one red and the other blue, to the left and right of the underside, and the two 'searchlight beams' were emanating from squarish-sectioned panels at the front. It hovered for a few minutes, and then started moving slowly to the northeast, passing 150 metres directly over their heads.

After pausing and hovering for a while longer, a bright red, evenly coloured, 'triangle' or 'cone' appeared just behind the craft, and increased in intensity. There was a 'swishing' noise, and the object accelerated upwards and away, at great speed, and disappeared into the northeast.

Kaikoura February 1993

It was only 6am, but already the crew of a small fishing trawler were out at sea, just off the mouth of the Clarence River. About one kilometre to their east a disc shaped craft suddenly shot out of the water. It was moving at a 'terrific speed' as zoomed up into to the sky, and shot off into the west, disappearing over the Kaikoura Ranges.

Tauranga Harbour 1st October 1993

Investigator Harvey Cooke reported on the following incident, which occurred at 8.15pm, when the witness and her friend were sitting at the kitchen table.

Through the window, they saw a very bright light, hovering in the sky, about 300 metres away. It formed a 'pyramid of light', going into the water, which, after about forty seconds, 'just sort of melted into the sea'.

The witness said; "There was no noise at all, not a sound, everything was so still, then it sort of turned off, and slowly descended in a half circle towards the house. By this time we were 'freaking'. As we had already turned out one light inside, my friend screamed out; "Turn off the other one!", which I did, as well as the TV.

"Her child was lying on the couch, terrified at what was going on, as she had seen it through the window on her side of the lounge. Then we just dashed to the lounge and huddled up, not knowing what was going to happen next."

They had yanked the curtains shut, but she lifted it up a bit, and could see that the object had come closer to the house, and was heading towards some trees approximately fifty metres away to the right.

She continued; "By this time it looked as though it had turned on its side, and just coasted around in front of us. It had two sets of lights, two blue at one end, and two red/pink ones at the other end. There was no real sound at all, just a low humming, buzzing noise."

After the object could no longer be seen, and hoping that it wouldn't return, the two women turned the lights and TV back on, and said they had never felt so scared of anything ever before. The witness, too frightened to go home on her own, stayed the night with her friend.

South Pacific June 1994

In the first week of June, the annual Regatta from New Zealand to Tonga, was, without warning, hit by one of the severest storms ever experienced. Many boats capsized, or became swamped or de-masted. As sailors, both professional and amateur, found themselves fighting for their lives, the New Zealand Navy and Air force, along with several private and commercial boats, set out on a desperate rescue mission.

As they plucked the helpless survivors, one by one, from the sea, their greatest problem was actually locating the stranded vessels in mountainous waves and unprecedented winds. The two man crew of the *'Ramtha'*, Australian Bill and Robyn Forbes, found themselves in desperate circumstances when their sails were stripped, and the steering mechanism broken.

The vessel, *'Monowai'*, was on its way to assist, however the crew could not position or spot the *'Ramtha'* in such terrible conditions. As the young couple clung to the bunks inside the small cabin, their attention was drawn to a bright illumination, hovering low in the sky above their boat. They could see a green orb of light twenty feet above the mast, however, it was later determined that none of the people involved in the rescue had launched a flare.

After some debate, the *'Monowai'* hastened to the location, and the Forbes couple were safely rescued. In a later documentary – *'Rescue South Pacific'* – *'Monowai'* Midshipman Tracy Kaio said; "It was the strangest thing I've ever seen. One minute it was pitch dark with driving rain, and our ship was doing 48 degree rolls in the enormous waves. Then suddenly everything changed. The sky lit up and we could see for miles. We were surrounded by green light, and the ocean seemed calm."

Sub-Lieutenant Andrew Saunderson added; "I've never seen anything so extraordinary. At first we thought it was a flare, but then the whole sky was blazing in bright emerald colours."

Another couple, Americans Divinie and Darryl Wheeler, along with their two children, were on board their catamaran *'Heart Light'*, when their boat began to break up in the heavy seas. The beam of light had also speared right down over their vessel, before moving on. They were also rescued, and Divinie, who claimed previous contact with aliens, was adamant that it was her extraterrestrial friends who had come to their, and the Forbes', aid.

Auckland 16th August 1996

The *'Connections'* publication reported on an unidentified object, seen, for over an hour, as it moved over the sky at Kohimarama, near Auckland. From the underside, it looked like an inverted saucer-shape, which was clearly illuminated from the intense strobing lights it was aiming at the ground. Every now and then it would send out 'balls' of light, and at one time it appeared to dispatch two smaller craft which it held in a beam of light.

A week later, more than fifty people witnessed a huge craft – estimated to be the size of three jumbo jets – as it hovered over Titirangi for nearly three-quarters-of-an-hour.

Near Auckland 15th February 1997

The shortwave station , *'Radio Pacific'*, reported that at 10am, several people in Takapuna reported a grey saucer passing overhead. The craft was perfectly visible in a sky that was clear except for a few broken clouds. Whilst the core appeared to remain stable, the outer rim was rotating or spinning.

The object had come from the direction of Auckland city, and flew on to the northwest. It headed out over the East Coast Bays toward Kawau Island.

South Island July 1997

Several campers, in the Mt. Evans area of the Tasman National Park, in the north-west corner of the South Island, got the shock of their lives at 6am one rainy morning. Coming up the gully, in their direction, was a diamond-shaped, metallic object, with several tripod-like legs. When it stopped to hover some eighty feet above the creek, they noticed that it was a windowed craft, with a central round light, which suddenly shone upon them.

Perhaps the occupants were also surprised, not expecting the presence of the campers. The lights 'switched off', and the craft rose silently into the air, and was lost from view behind some trees.

Christchurch 12th November 1997

At 7.40am, a Port Hills resident saw two most unusual oval-shaped objects travelling from south to north across the sky, at an altitude of about 3,500ft. He estimated their speed as being eighty to one hundred miles per hour, and each would have been about twelve metres in diameter.

His description of the strange craft was a little different from that normally given; *"The UFOs appeared to be shaped like human eyes. In the centre was a silver ball, and the outer areas were black, and tapered off to a point. The objects travelled above light cloud in a blue sky, and there were heavy gusts of wind at the time.'*

Tauranga 15th November 1997

At 9.50pm, a couple both saw a UFO flying over Welcome Bay, about one hundred metres away from where they were standing on a second storey veranda, looking north. It was a round shape, almost misty in appearance, and approximately fifteen to twenty feet in diameter. There was no noise or lights, and it disappeared from view after a few seconds.

Auckland 26th November 1999

'MUFON's' George Filer published an interesting report from Jason Monds, who was on holiday on the North Island. As it was a hot night, at 11.30pm, he and some friends were heading to a remote beach for a swim.

Just before they reached the sand, they saw a silent, cigar-shaped object moving very rapidly up and down the shore. It had a strange glistening, silver appearance, and seemed to mysteriously disappear, then 're-materialize' at a different point.

As Jason and his friend Andrew, who were a bit braver than their companions, crept closer, and moved up the beach towards the object. It had paused, and was hovering about five hundred metres off shore. Jason was not happy when Andrew picked up a few shells, and threw them at the object. Wilbur, Andrew's dog, who had accompanied them, was barking and running forwards into the water every time the craft moved.

After they had watched for about ten minutes, Jason wanted to leave, but Andrew insisted on grabbing Wilbur, who was still in the water, barking. He said that as he entered the water and reached out to get hold of his dog, he felt a strange gravity or static energy run through him.

With Wilbur safely 'in tow', they raced back up the beach, and looked back. The strange craft, which was now about one hundred metres above the water, suddenly gained altitude. It dematerialized again, but this time seemed to disappear completely, leaving nothing but a strange shimmer in its place.

When they returned to the rest of their group, one of the girls, Jess, was hysterical, and had already rung the police, who turned up about an hour later, but the strange craft was long gone.

Jason further reported; *'Bethell's Beach is regarded by the local natives as a highly spiritual area and scientists have found massive concentrations of iron in the sand, giving it a black or purple appearance. I spoke to Manu, a New Zealand native Maori, who has lived on the beach for thirty years. He claims UFOs are a regular occurrence, and that he'd actually made contact with the craft's occupants on several occasions. He said that in Maori legend, the natives had actually been guided by the 'sea beings' to New Zealand on their journey from the Hawaiian Islands, long before white people had arrived.'*

North Island 15th December 1999

The *'Ufologist'* magazine received several reports from *'MUFON NZ'* and *'TUFOIG'*. One told of a commercial pilot who, at about 11.30pm, was walking with a friend on a beach located on the east coast. A large, green light came across the water, and silently accelerated past the witnesses at an estimated 200 knots and an altitude of about one hundred feet. They watched as it travelled a further three kilometres before disappearing.

'The pilot later spoke to a nearby farmer who told him that he had observed a similar event while driving his tractor. The farmer had topped a rise, and suddenly stopped his tractor when he saw a huge UFO fifty metres away.

'There were flashing lights around a middle rim of a stationary disc which was one hundred metres in diameter. The farmer turned off his lights, and at that moment the lights on the object also went out. Another bright light appeared at the top, and it took off with a deep buzzing noise and disappeared.'

Christchurch 29th July 2000

Kevin Emmett loved taking his five-year-old son onto the back patio every night, where he taught him about the stars and the universe. This particular night, they had just gone outside, when there was a bright flash across the sky.

At first Kevin thought it was sheet lightning, but then a 'standard disc-shaped craft' flew right over their home, and headed towards the hills. His frightened son ran inside, whilst Kevin and his wife watched through binoculars as the object did a quick U-turn, and flew back in the direction from whence it came.

New Plymouth 1st January 2001

Diane Harrison from '*AUFORN*' was contacted by five witnesses who were in a car, driving down Highway-3 on the west coast of the North Island. It was just after midnight, and the start of the New Year, when their radio developed a static 'buzz'. A little further down the road, they realised that there was 'something orange' hovering above the car.

They all got out of the car, and could see an object, hovering about one hundred feet overhead. It was silent, and appeared to be circular, with a diameter between thirty to fifty feet. They looked around, and noticed three other objects, hovering and swaying around in the air. They seemed to be changing colour, from metallic, glowing orange to metallic deep purple and shades of blue.

Suddenly, a larger object appeared on the horizon, and sped towards the other four. The witness said; *'Each seemed to react in a way similar to an army unit, and formed a line and disappeared almost instantly towards Mount Taranaki.'*

Waiheke Island 13th July 2001

Not much is known about any activity on the Island since the departure of the 'visitors' in the 1980s, however, this particular afternoon, at 5.30pm, Anthony Milas and his girlfriend saw a grey cigar-shaped object, with a trailing flame, moving slowly downwards, and arcing to the north.

After five minutes, it broke into two trails, one larger than the other. The small one appeared to hover, whilst the larger object, which had been travelling fairly fast, slowed its descent, and moved to the north, before disappearing, after about five minutes, behind some cloud near Rangitoto Island.

August 2001

By the turn of the century, the incidences of hoaxes, often perpetrated by college and university students, were on the rise. The *'Timaru Herald'* was only one of the provincial newspapers to condemn what was essentially a dangerous practise.

Balloons made of plastic rubbish bags, wire and firelighters, floated overhead, and usually crash landed in a paddock. The students were 'stoked' at the furore they had caused, but the authorities were not impressed, and threatened further punitive action if the pranks continued.

Fire Safety Officer, Kevin Collins noted that twice in the past couple of years, students had ended up in court in Timaru. In one incident a telephone box had been blown up, and in the other two students received suspended prison sentences and were ordered to pay reparation of $6,000 each after starting a fire on the landing of a two storey house while there were ten people inside.

Kakitaki, Bay of Plenty, August 2002

'UFOCUS' interviewed multiple excited reports from two classrooms of college students at Kakatiki, when during one afternoon's lessons, a white, teardrop-shape 'cloud' was seen falling or descending vertically from the sky, above the outskirts of the township, about a kilometre away.

As they watched the relatively slow and controlled movement of the unusual 'cloud', they noticed that protruding from the bottom was a rounded, shiny, metallic shape which reflected sunlight as it moved slightly from side to side.

They realised that the 'teardrop' shaped 'cloud' was actually a 'misty' substance, streaming upwards off the outer edges of the object.

Some of the observers thought it must be a helicopter on fire, and braced themselves for an expected 'crash', which never eventuated. Instead, the strange object came to a halt above some treetops, where it hovered momentarily before shooting back up, at a low angle, into the clear blue sky. Whilst above the trees, the surrounding 'mist' had dissipated, and a metallic-type 'shape' could be distinctly seen. Everybody was in agreement that the rate of descent had been to slow for that of a plane, and its subsequent speed of ascent, back into the sky, was much too fast for any helicopter to achieve.

Eight days later, *'UFOCUS'* received a call from a woman who lived twenty kilometres to the south of Kakatiki. At 10am that morning, she had witnessed a similar event. She looked out of her window to see what she thought was a helicopter about to crash into a nearby paddock.

An object with a rounded, silver, metallic undercarriage, which was glinting in the sun, had appeared to be falling rapidly from high in the sky. Clouds of what she thought was white smoke were streaming from the lower sides of the craft, surrounding it with a 'teardrop' shape cloud, similar to that which had been seen by the college students. She looked out, but could hear no sound of an engine or rotor blades.

As had occurred on the previous occasion, the craft came to an abrupt halt, and hovered in the sky for a few seconds, before rapidly shooting off to the west and the Kaimai Ranges. By this time, as before, the 'cloud' had dissipated, and the object was visibly a metallic craft with a short contrail.

Nelson 11th June 2004

On the evening of 11th June, a teardrop-shaped, metallic craft, with spinning red lights, was seen beaming light onto the water. It made a humming sound, and residents could also hear an occasional thundering boom. Moving at phenomenal speed, it appeared and disappeared in various places. At one point, before it moved off, back into the sky, it came close to the beach, sending beams of light across Ruby Bay.

Over the next hour, six craft, which looked like giant orbs of amber light, appeared in the sky, and moved around the area. Some, which randomly came in close before shooting off again, didn't disappear until dawn. Many of the camping ground residents also saw them, and the next morning, several found that their car batteries were 'flat', and dead fish were mysteriously being washed up on the beach.

A more unusual report was received by '*MUFON's* George Filer in 2004. On the afternoon of July 21st, a farmer saw a disc-shaped craft flying over. Later that night, he and a friend saw a bright, cream coloured light, and when they looked out, there was a hovering disc-shaped craft, with rock-like projectiles on the outside surface.

They ran out into the paddock when they saw a neon blue beam shining onto the ground. The farmer stated that they had run back into the house when rocks started falling onto the ground. He said; "There was a big flash, and that's all I remember about that night!

"The next morning I went out to check upon the calves, and there were slaughtered heifers scattered on the ground. The craft, which had made a sound like a chainsaw cutting through a log, had given a magnetic effect on all the metals in a 100-metre vicinity, including our barbed wire fence."

(Perhaps the 'visitors' were not so friendly anymore!)

Tauranga 23rd February 2006

Suzy Hanson investigated the following incident, which occurred at 11pm, when a 26-year-old male saw-mill operator was walking home after visiting friends;

'It was a warm, still evening. The sky was very clear and cloudless... and stars visible....he noticed three oval lights approaching in a triangular formation, moving from south to north at an estimated eighty kms/hr. The lights looked strange, as although they were bright, they were not diffusive or radiating light. They appeared to be very low – below 500 feet, but despite this, the witness could not make out any form or outline of an object. His initial thought was that it was an aircraft, however he realised there was no sound at all.

'As the lights came closer, he saw they were large, circular and bright yellow/white. He described them as; "Like bright dinner plates – flat, not sending out a beam or glow of light, but still extremely bright." The formation was "bigger than a car, but smaller than a house."

'He became apprehensive when the lights changed configuration as they came closer and passed overhead. The two rear lights moved forward diagonally, and merged with the leading light, briefly becoming one, before moving back to the triangular formation. The witness said; "It was brief – you could see an 'after blur' of the movement. He watched the objects continue silently on their course, repeating this pattern until they were no longer visible.'

'UFOCUS NZ' determined that there were no scheduled aircraft in the area at the time when both Tauranga and Rororua airports were closed. Further, the military advised that no military craft were operational in the area that night, and neither were there any SAS manoeuvres, which didn't commence until the following weeks.

North Island March 2007

March 2007 was a busy month for Suzy Hanson and the investigators at *'UFOCUS'*. At 10.30pm on 8th March, two hunters on a volcanic plateau next to Mt. Ruapehu, noticed about eighty hectares of scrub land which had been burnt down to the dirt. When they looked back down on it, they could see a strange display of lights, roughly at, or just above, ground level. They stopped their vehicle, in order to get a better view.

A trapezium-shaped object was being illuminated by four evenly spaced bright red/orange lights, and a larger yellowish light above. Since the witnesses had differing opinions as to what they were seeing, one jumped out and shone a spotlight onto the area. Immediately, the lights went out, and the object, which was 'bigger than a bus', silently took off into the sky, and swiftly exited in a southerly direction, at a very low altitude.

Three days later, on 11th March, a witness reported a rectangular box-shaped object in the sky over Rotorua. Five days after that, at 11pm, on 16th March, two women standing in the driveway of one's house, on the outskirts of Tauranga, saw a rectangular object, 'the size of a bus or larger' in the sky.

It was glowing an amber/orange, and moving slowly, and silently eastward above the treetops beyond the subdivision. At first its shape appeared to be rectangular, but as it moved higher, they could see that its sides were sloped at an angle, similar to a trapezium. At one stage, it briefly tilted, and they could see what resembled an oval shape on top. It moved out over the sea, and was soon lost from view in the cloud. Air Traffic Control later confirmed to investigators that there were no known aircraft over that area at the time of the sighting.

Rototuna North – Hamilton 31st January 2009

Suzy Hanson also investigated this incident, which occurred at 9.45pm when the witness was standing in his back garden, just looking up at the clear night sky. He noticed a couple of white lights, moving towards him, in tandem, and on a downwards path.

As they silently, and smoothly passed overhead, and across the roof of his house, he realised that there were three lights, positioned at three points on an isosceles-shaped triangular object. The craft, which had a dark brown underside, reflecting the city lights, continued on towards the north and Hamilton.

Later investigations determined that the object would have been at an altitude of 800-1,000ft, and travelling at approximately 100 to 120 mph.

CHAPTER NINE

CONTACTEES AND EXPERIENCERS

The subject of contactees and experiencers is complex and multifaceted, and even today, we still have much to learn and understand.

Brinsley le Poer Trench jumped on the bandwagon with his *'Contact'* groups, where at specific times several people together would concentrate on the space visitors. Whilst often a lot of mumbo-jumbo would come out of these experiments, occasionally meaningful and intelligent communication would eventuate.

Sometimes people encountered extraterrestrials without even knowing it. This brought to mind, a letter I have, which was sent to New Zealand researcher, Fred Dickeson. In *'The Days of the Space Brothers'*, I detail George Adamski's 1959 tour of New Zealand. It was said that two of the 'brothers' quietly accompanied him, and used to slip into the back of the hall after he started his lecture. Some UFO enthusiasts had been told that they had actually met and spoken with one of the 'Brothers' without even realising it.

One of the audience, a local group member, was vigilant in trying to identify the 'visitors', and one night he spotted a possible contender. He reached into his bag, pulled out his camera, and directed it to the suspected fellow sitting at the rear of the audience. Suddenly, the man started to disappear, from the feet up. The witness's photo clearly displayed only the upper half of the man's torso!

There were other incidents in New Zealand, many of which were not reported until many years later. Some were never reported, due to New Zealand society being more conservative than some in other parts of the world.

Investigator, Suzy Hanson, related a couple of episodes, when the experiencers did not confide in her until late in life.

In 1941, Margaret, the eldest of ten children, was only eight years old when they lived in a rural part of Hawkes Bay. One night, Margaret was lying in bed, and she could see, through the window, a large, bright bluish/white light, descending towards Te Mata peak.

In those days, there were no helicopters, and it moved around, as if seeking a landing spot, however the area below was rugged terrain, and impossible for a conventional plane. It went out of sight behind a hill, and then reappeared, swooped around the Peak, and slowly went down into the valley. Slowly and silently it smoothly descended and landed in a farm paddock across the road.

Margaret got out of bed and looked out of the window. She saw a 'soccer ball' size blue light, which emerged from the larger one and flew rapidly over the paddock and road, towards her bedroom window. As it reached her, the light entered Margaret's room, enveloping her. She experienced something akin to an explosion, and remembered no more.

The next morning, when her mother didn't believe her, Margaret went over to the paddock, and found a large circular area of swirled and flattened grass where she had seen the light descend the night before.

In 1943, when Margaret was ten, she stayed with friends in a nearby valley whilst her parents were away. The situation became more sinister when she awoke one morning to find blood on her underwear and the sheets. She did not reach puberty for another three years, and whilst it appeared that no harm had been done, the following night she was afraid to go to sleep, in case 'something or someone' came to take her away, as she could remember a figure bending over her.

It is not known if this incident was due to a criminal human act, or related to a history, known mainly by investigators, of young girls being abducted and subjected to gynaecological procedures prior to puberty.

Since that incident, Margaret felt that some unknown 'someone or something' has been protecting her from harm. Often she has heard a 'telepathic voice' or had a psychic premonition which has saved her from impending danger.

In the 1960s, when in her late twenties, Margaret developed a large abscess in her ear, and when it drained, a small, off-white, hard bone-like object came out of the infected site. It was about 5mm long and 2-3mm wide, barrel-shaped, with a protruding point or prong extending from each end.

One evening, she had a sudden, short, 'flashback' memory of two strange beings, with wrinkled faces and large black eyes, and also of descending down a 'tunnel' into a bright place, where a small 'glowing boy' took hold of her hands and spoke to her.

In another 'flashback' she recalled another night when she was only ten, and had a clear memory of an object in the paddock. It was spherical and metallic, floating just above the ground, and had a bright bluish/white light emanating from what appeared to be windows on the upper third of the craft. There was a small, thin, helmeted figure, wearing something like a backpack, next to the craft.

Unfortunately, 'flashbacks' do unexpectedly occur, as if there has been some form of memory suppression, which sometimes malfunctions. It can leave the subject both confused and curious as the what, if anything, had happened to them.

———————————————

Suzy spoke of another witness who described what had occurred in 1956, on a stud farm near Waipukurau.

The witness, Ann Kebbell, was only eighteen at the time, and one night, in late June, she and her family saw a small, silver-grey, saucer-shaped object which hovered, about fifty yards away, and twenty feet up, over the land between their cowshed and a line of pine trees. It was similar to the length of a car in width, and emitted a very bright light, which illuminated the surrounding paddocks.

For the previous six weeks, there had been reports of UFOs in the Hawke's Bay area, but they hadn't expected anything like this. Ann said her family seemed transfixed whilst she was terrified, and jumped around behind her father.

Their grazing sheep seemed unperturbed, but the dogs went berserk, howling and straining on their chains, as if trying to get away. After a few minutes, the craft rose quickly back into the sky, stopped, changed direction, and disappeared in a flash.

Ann's family, although amazed by the incident, did not seem to be affected. Ann, however, shook uncontrollably for some hours after, and developed a severe headache which didn't go away until the next day.

"After this experience my Father swore us to secrecy and we were not to mention any of it to anyone for fear of being a laughing stock of the community. However, Dad did take me into his confidence, and told me that he had seen things in the sky before, and said that the next afternoon he would show me some of them in daylight.

"True to his word, they were sitting above the horizon of the hills that were part of my brother's farm. There were three that were sitting on their sides amidst the clouds. They looked like zinc coloured objects as opposed to the light fluffy clouds around them.

"I have often wondered what else Dad had experienced that he did not share with us."

I, and other researchers, also wonder. Whilst this time no occupants were actually sighted, the craft was obviously under intelligent control.

BETTY

Sometimes, we will never know the extent of a contactee's interaction with extraterrestrial intelligence.

Born in 1946, Betty was raised in Bondi and had a traumatic childhood resulting in nervousness and learning disabilities. Betty, like her mother, is psychic and as a child 'saw' things. She suppressed these abilities for a long time, but now practises as a psychic medium – sensitive to audio, visual and touch. Ever since she was a child she can hear sounds – like 'frequencies'.

In 1964 she spent a year on a working holiday in New Zealand, and was employed at and living in a hotel at Waitomo Caves. Just after she had been out with a caving group she went to bed at 11pm Friday night. She wasn't ill, but stirred on Saturday afternoon, then did not wake or remember anything until Sun afternoon 4-5pm. Betty feels it odd that she has never forgotten this, despite her abilities later in life.

She often had strange dreams – like it was a 'medium' experience – looking through a 'veil' with the spirits on the other side, maybe in another dimension. In about 2006 she was living in Parramatta when she woke up in bed – she doesn't know why, but was fully awake and not dreaming. She saw a 'veil' – as if between two worlds – but this time it was opening and she could see what looked like a laboratory, with lab equipment that seemed to be 'floating molecules'. She was very frightened and kept thinking that 'aliens' would 'step through' or walk out and get her. She closed her eyes in fear and 'went out like a light' – not waking up until the next morning.

Whilst she has inter-dimensional connections, she always considered it on the spiritual side, but when in a writers' group she suddenly had a compulsion to compose a story about UFOs. Betty had never attended any UFO meetings until a friend told her about a 'get-together' that I run. She felt an inexplicable compulsion to come, and later confided in me.

Betty felt that something she cannot consciously remember had happened to her, either in New Zealand or at some other time. She initially indicated that she would like me to arrange a regressive hypnosis session to find out, but then hesitated and retreated back into her protective shell. Often possible witnesses or contactees are torn between wanting to know or pretending nothing happened.

These sightings of strange craft and their occupants, were coming from all over the world. In my books, 'Contact Down Under', 'The Alien Gene', and 'The Days of the Space Brothers', I wrote about several from New Zealand.

Waiheke Island

Looking into the history of Waiheke Island, just off Auckland on the N.Z. coast, one realises it was an ideal location for clandestine experiments – as a remote, sub-tropical island, only a short ferry ride to Auckland. It is hilly, (Mount Maunganui is 231 metres high), nineteen kilometres long, and varies from 0.64 to 9.65 kilometres wide. Originally occupied by the Maori, it has a long history of bloody tribal battles. The first Europeans set foot there in 1801, but white settlers only arrived in 1830.

The population was sparse, only numbering 835 at the end of World War 2. A few years earlier a network of tunnels and gun emplacements was constructed to defend the eastern side of Auckland Harbour; it is possibly that at this time its potential was recognised. Residents remain few – 2,144 in1955, 3,500 in 1978, 4,554 in 1986 – by which time the main facility, which Patty described, had shut down.

There were few local government structures or services, and building constructions have been unregulated and unsupervised. There was no full local government until 1970, and very little oversight until amalgamated with Auckland in 1989. It would have been easy for any quasi-government or military agency to bring equipment, supplies and provisions in, without attracting much attention from authorities or the locals.

Islands are an ideal location for these types of secret facilities – hidden away from public scrutiny and difficult to access!

In *'The Alien Gene'* I discuss the events on Waiheke Island. In the 1970s several islanders witnessed many visitations by, and had contact with, humanoid aliens who were working with scientists on a secret project. Patty, one of the contactees, said that sometimes the 'visitors' would walk around, unrecognised, in the town. The project closed down later, when Waiheke's population increased, and as the children reached adulthood, many left the island.

My investigations, and research into this entire scenario commenced in 2000, when I met Becky who worked in a local shop. As we became friends and she learnt of my UFO research work, she decided to confide in me about the odd events her family had experienced in New Zealand, and the reason they had moved to Australia and settled in the Blue Mountains. She was concerned about recent incidents which involved her daughter, Patricia.

She couldn't say very much with customers around, and suggested we meet with 'Patty', who could fill us in on some of the details. Fellow researcher Bryan Dickeson and I met her in Katoomba, and I visited Patty later at her house in Lawson. Her lifelong friend Gillian and Patty's boyfriend, Mark, were also there, and over the months and years of friendship that followed, it became apparent that an amazing series of encounters had affected not just Becky's family, but many others as well.

What made this case so interesting, from an investigator's viewpoint, was that most of the witnesses had not read UFO literature, or attended any meetings or conferences on the subject. Becky was in denial, and if she had experienced anything she refused to discuss it, and eventually moved to a property in Western New South Wales. (This was interesting, given that many experiencers felt the urge to move away from the coast and become self-sufficient.)

Becky's ex-husband James, (Patty's father), was certainly deeply involved in 'aliens', but not influenced by outside information or the media. They were all very concerned about recent contacts in Australia, but I managed to get them to start from the beginning, in New Zealand.

Patty and Gillian were in their late twenties and early thirties. They met and became good friends as children on Waiheke Island, in the Hauraki Gulf, some miles east of Auckland, New Zealand. Patty was born in London in 1972, and migrated to New Zealand as a child with her parents, to join family on the Island, in 1974.

Gillian was born in Naples, Italy, in 1962, and her father, who was in the Italian Navy during the War, was from a seafaring family, with an added mixture of Scottish and gypsy heritage, from her British mother. (It was much later, when I researched their family history that I found similarities to other 'experiencers', and thought to myself, 'here we go again'!)

Gillian started to explain. "We migrated to New Zealand in 1965, when I was three, and lived first in an isolated cottage in the central North Island – an area they call the King Country. It's funny, I can't remember many details of my life before the age of nine, except that there were strange events and energies, which affected my mother. I used to sense that 'energy' and often felt frightened in the house. I have this sense of 'feelings' and knowing that more happened, but just cannot recall it no matter how hard I try. I have been told that there are very powerful energies in the area, which is apparently prone to UFO activity.

"We moved to Waiheke Island when I was about eleven. We lived in a semi-rural area again. About two kilometres away was this huge property, which took up all of one headland. It was supposed to be a farm, a sort of 'New Age' place owned by two wealthy Americans, L.P. and M.W. They were overseas some of the time, and their farm manager, Jack MacKay, was specially brought out from Scotland to manage the property. In fact, L.P. chose all staff," she reflected.

"L.P. lived in the main house, and M.W. in the homestead just below. It was difficult to access the house; one side was on the edge of a cliff going down to the sea, and the other had lots of dips and hollows. A third cottage nearby was also connected with L.P. and M.W. This was always closed up with darkened windows; the locals said it must hold something secret, or be some kind of gathering place."

(It is of interest that the building was on a headland. The cliffs below, going down to the sea, could hide the arrival, and possible entry, of all manner of craft, whether they were on the water or in the air!)

Gillian explained her own connection to the farm: "My mother got some casual employment there, and when she babysat for the L.P. family, we usually stayed overnight, sometimes for a few days. Occasionally Patty stayed with us as well. There were three children – an eighteen-month baby, Paul, a girl of four or five, and son Max, who was incredibly intelligent. It was whispered he was being groomed for something, but I don't know what.

"The place was sometimes referred to as a 'farm stay', but the locals were always suspicious and whispered it was a cover for something else. A lot of extra stuff had been specially added. They built an odd, large landing pad, supposedly for helicopters, but no-one ever once saw or heard a chopper coming!"

(Becky, Patty's mother told me there had been strange comings and goings to the farm as far back as the 1950s. She named some well-known people from overseas: "Originally L.P. had claimed he was going to build a community, but of course, this never happened.)"

Gillian continued, "There was an office which I wasn't allowed to go into, and it was all very secretive. Sometimes I would see the door open and strange, non-local, scientific looking people would come in and out, usually with L.P. or M.W. Through the door I caught glimpses of banks of electronic equipment which seemed to have cables going out the window.

"There was a locked basement downstairs, which L.P. said contained 'his stuff', and I wasn't allowed to go there either." She paused, "I can still remember. The stairwell was dark and foreboding, but one night I noticed the door at the bottom was open, and nobody around. I ignored my fears and snuck down. Once inside I was amazed. I saw square boards of machines with dials, knobs, indicator lights and cables. There were technology screens, like something out of 'Star Trek'. I was nervous about breaking the rules and going in, when I suddenly saw what I can only describe as a shadow of something or someone, which seemed to be fleeing for cover. I got out of there very quickly, and from then on was always scared of going downstairs near that basement.

"I was even a little afraid of sleeping in the guest room, and would sometimes hear a continual steady, background humming noise. One night we heard a noise, like a loud detonation. It was not a gunshot, more like a deep resonating boom above the house. It shook the whole place. There seemed to be strange vibes all around the back part of the house.

"It was what happened, a short time later, that really freaked me out," she faltered. "Max came running into my mother, saying; "Paul is weird. He's laughing and talking in a deep voice." Mum told me to stay in bed, and she spent the rest of the night in Paul's room."

Gillian left Waiheke in 1979-80 and didn't return for 20 years. She and Patty, who had a very strong 'psychic' bond, remained in contact the entire time.

Patty told me about her life on the Island, which even today, she thinks of as 'home'; "As a child, looking back now, my life seems to be a blur. There seems to be pieces of my childhood missing somehow. At the age of about two or three I did spend some time living on the 'farm' when my parents were away. Gillian and her mother were also there looking after the children.

"I have fond memories of the Island, and remember spending most of my time with my grandparents. I loved being with them, it seemed routine to live half my time with my parents, and the other half with my grandparents, who lived in the rural area. In fact, my grandmother also came to Australia and the Blue Mountains with us."

Patty recounted events during her childhood: "I have always been curious about the unknown, even when very young, and often looked up at the stars and dreamt of faraway places. When I was four, I was staying with my grandparents, and probably asleep in bed at the time, (my grandmother told me about this many years later). She and my uncle were watching television when all power in the house went dead. They were sitting in complete darkness, and thought a fuse might have blown. When they looked out, they realised it was a blackout as they could not see any normal street and house lights shining in the distance.

"They went outside. They could hear an unusual humming, and smelt a strange fume-like odour of some kind. Down in the valley Gran could see a circular object with lights all around it. She said it couldn't have been a house because there were no homes in that area. To this day, Gran is sure it was an unidentified flying object."

'Gran', who spent her final days in Australia, in the Blue Mountains, confirmed this for me, and insists that a flying saucer had landed in the valley below. "That was not all," Gran said, "A few days later a strange woman came to my door, and asked if she could come in. I think she was European, she looked and sounded as if she was Swedish or similar. She wanted me to join a meditation group at the 'farm', and when I told her 'No', she played me a tape. It was the strangest music, a mixture of squeaking and humming. She said it was a communication from another world."

Partly from her partially 'missing time', filled in when under hypnosis, Patty recalled an event from Waiheke Island at about the same young age. She woke in bed one night when a blue light was coming through the closed window. She had 'seen this light before' and got up to look through the curtains. The whole house was surrounded in a brilliant blue light. She couldn't believe it, but was not worried as her 'Friend' was coming with several of his small companions.

She saw him appear within the blue light, and then he came through her window into the room, which was flooded in blue. He was accompanied by six or seven 'little people' – small, with medium-sized, oval-shaped heads, creamy-brown skin and big black eyes 'like dark mirrors.' They were not much taller than Patty, and had long, skinny arms with four fingers, but no thumb, on each hand. Her Friend was much, much taller. They were all wearing a similar, neck high full-body suit, which was a blue-grey shiny material, like a wet suit, with a red triangular motif on the right-hand side.

Once in the room, her Friend bent down to her and put out both his hands. He looked down and she placed her hands just above his, without actually touching. "He spoke to me, but his mouth didn't move. I felt good, and wasn't worried, when he explained we would always be friends, and not to be afraid.

"I knew that sometimes they took me up into the space ship above the house, and this time I was going there to play with the little people. The small ones stepped into the blue light, which covered the roof of the whole house, followed by me and my Friend. I felt good and relaxed, and it shrank, like a spotlight, as we went up."

Patty's next memory was of being on board the craft; "The little people were around me, running around and chasing each other, playing tag or something like that. I had seen them before, they were always there. I was more interested in a strange lady who had just walked in.

"She looked different to my Friend, more human-like. Her face was like the aliens, with a small mouth, two dots for a nose, and no lips, but she had very blue human eyes and long, white straggly hair. She was wearing a long, white loose robe, and had browny-cream coloured skin with normal human-type hands.

"She was scary, and seemed angry, looking at me as if I shouldn't be there. I had never seen her before, and as she walked away I think my Friend was having an argument with her. I kept playing with the little people, and after a while she went off down a corridor. My Friend came back, and calmed me down with 'feelings'. (He could communicate feelings without actually saying anything.)"

As with other experiencers, Patty had described entering the craft through a 'porthole' in the floor; "There were a series of very big octagonal rooms, on the same level, joined together by a series of corridors. After the nasty lady left, my Friend took me into one. There were four blank walls behind us, and we were facing the other four which had big screens.

"He had brought the little ones with us, perhaps to take our minds off the big argument. My Friend turned the screens on and showed me so many pictures; lots and lots of stars and galaxies. It was so much to take in all at once, different planets, somewhere else, not here! At first, I thought they were taking me away, it seemed I was being 'drawn in', moving through space, with stars going by. Really strange!

"We arrived at an unusual place, which I think was his home planet. The landscape was mostly red dirt, with a prehistoric look about it. Everything was big, with lots of strange desert plants, big multicoloured leaves, which apparently ate insects. There were lots of concrete buildings, which looked like huts, but they had connecting tunnels. My Friend told me that it was too hot for them to live outside.

"Inside, everything was round and bright white. The windows were triangular, but although tinted, still had light streaming through. I saw a see-through glass or plastic table with stools all around, and I was shown metallic capsules, which shut when they go inside to sleep. I was told they don't sleep much and only eat infrequently."

Patty said the experience was weird. She was there, she could see and feel everything, but not actually touch anything.

"He took me to his house, and I met his family. His wife was a bit shorter than him, no hair, but softer skin and normal body with two small breasts noticeable beneath her clothes. She seemed nice, not like that other nasty lady. He had two children, a little boy and a little girl, who looked identical but had different characteristics. They all wore the same blue-grey outfit with the red triangle motif.

"We played different games, some on the screen, some running around, and one with different coloured balls which floated. There were solid balls and others that were more ethereal. After saying goodbye my Friend took me by the hand and led me away."

As she was undergoing regressive hypnosis, Patty's description of the next experience was a little childish. He told her it was time to go home and they then went back through the tunnels and entered "a big, big, big, big room where there are lots of ships. "The ships are round and they've got – they're huge. This one – it's round like a saucer and shiny, metallic, very reflective. It's like a place where you keep planes. It's huge, like a big cave."

Patty's Friend then took her back home – through the blue light and her bedroom window. Once he put her back into bed he left. The next morning, she did have some memory of the event, which faded soon afterwards.

I was interested to know more about Patty's 'Friend', and how long he had been part of her life. Later, under hypnosis, Patty recalled an event from Waiheke Island when she was about three- and-a-half years old.

"We were at the 'homestead' having breakfast. We always had breakfast there every weekend and there were lots of children and adults present. My Dad was there but my Mum didn't like these occasions.

"I can see all the people – the group we were in. M.W. was there, other parents, and a visiting artist – a painter. My Dad was sitting out on the porch and I was in the garden making daisy chains. The chooks were all around me – it was a wonderful time.

"All my little friends, my friends, four other children, went running into the neighbouring bushland because there's a path up to the house on the top of the hill. We were running along this path, playing hide-and-seek, I could see a strange figure standing behind a tree. I was on the pathway, looking out into the bush and he's peeking, poking his head around the corner.

"I've never seen a head like that before. It's got big black eyes, like a mirror black; he's very tall and he's talking to me – in my mind. He's telling me not to be afraid; we've been doing this a long time: 'I'm your friend, can I play?' I feel that I have met him, that I know him.

"He started playing with all of us, just joined in with all the children. They all know him too. We're walking, making our way up to the other house on the top of the hill. He's with us, leading up to the house. It's still morning.

"I can see something. It's like a strange saucer-shaped thing on the ground nearby, next to the house, on the ground. It's got, like 'spikes', coming out from underneath it and these hold it up from the ground. It's roundish, mainly, a bit under twenty feet across, to the right of the house and slightly down the hill, near the flying fox. I think I've seen something like that before – it doesn't look 'alien' to me for some reason. It doesn't worry me at all, and our tall 'leader' is very nice.

"The kids are all playing on the flying fox up near the craft. Then these little people come out of the disc-like object. They're shorter than my Friend. Taller than me, but very small compared to him. They're very little – they look like little children. I think I've seen people like them before, and I don't feel worried at all.

"There are four other children –and about six of the little people. Gillian is there too. She's up at the big house, keeping an eye on us from time to time – she looks after us; she looks out for us. She's the only one there; all the other adults are down at the homestead, after breakfast.

"We're laughing a lot and running around and they're taking us into the little disc. There's a little, flat ramp that comes from underneath and an open door into the centre of the disc from the bottom. The four spikes that keep the disc off the ground are quite solid, metallic.

"The craft is completely metallic and there are oval windows – windows all round. It's like a disc, and then there's a rounder lump, or dome, on top which has the little oval windows all round that. It's like two deep saucers one on top of the other, but quite small. The little people are in there already. Then my Friend is leading the way, followed by me and then my friends. It's quite cramped so the little people are moving aside to give us room.

"Inside it's like – it's very small and round. There's one seat in the middle of the room, a black seat, with no controls. There's one screen in front of the seat. And there's a window in front of that. The screen thing has lights inside it, but it doesn't have any controls.

"We're all standing inside the craft and I'm looking at the seat and screen. There are small bench seats behind the central black seat. We're all inside, looking around. It's got an open grating-type floor too. You can see through that to something that's underneath – it's probably the 'engine room' area. We're so small that it seems big, but it's not very big at all.

"We had all wanted to see inside the craft, to 'have a look', because it seemed interesting. The chair, which has a leather-type of feel, is just like an office chair, but there are screens on the arms, where you put your hands. I sat in the chair for a while, but they don't really want the children to play with the screens at all – they say it could be dangerous, 'We're only little.'

"We were all looking around and playing – not asking questions at all, we're just interested and want to play with things, but we're not really allowed to. There's nothing on the screen; it's all 'shut black.' The oval windows have shutters down on them or something, so you can't see through them. They say that when you fly, you can see through them.

"They're explaining that they come from a very, very long way away. (Patty's new Friend is explaining all this.) 'They've been doing this for a very long time. They've been visiting us for a long time. Don't be afraid. They are friends with my Dad's friends.'

"We are not worried, just laughing and playing and looking around. They must know my father's friends, because they're at the house – They've got their spaceship parked there.

When the children got bored, they went back down the ramp to the flying fox to play. The Friend and his small people just watched them from near the craft.

Occasionally, Patty looks over towards the space craft, but she is mostly playing on the flying fox: "It's still there – they just watch us and some of the little people go back inside the disc."

Later, Patty could see all the other adults coming up the track from the homestead – the spaceship was still there. They come up the path and seem to know her new Friend. They talk to him. The children are still playing on the flying fox and the adults stand around in a circle, near the Friend and talk. Patti's father, M.W., L.P., and the parents are all there – just talking.

Then all the adults go into the house, with the Friend. They're in the house for a long time; "The kids are on the flying fox – there's so much to do"!

"There are a couple of little people inside the disc, working on something. There are four in the house, but none near the flying fox. Two 'little people' are under the spaceship –they've gone inside it, underneath, doing something. There's a hatch, near the main access door – they climb in there and they're not coming out."

After a good while Patty's father came out of the house, down the path towards the flying fox and said that they had to go home now. The space craft was still there with the little people inside the hatch. Patty's new Friend came out of the house to say 'Goodbye' and Patty and her father headed down the track, back towards the homestead. Occasionally Patty looked back to see her Friend standing there, watching them leave. There were no little people visible, but Patty said M.W. also came out of the house to wave goodbye.

Patty and her father went back down to the homestead where her father's car was parked outside in the driveway. They could see the house on top of the hill but not the spacecraft at all – it was parked slightly down the hill in 'a bit of a dip', well-obscured from the road.

Patty and her father drove home, but didn't tell her mother anything about it.

After describing the recovered memories, Patty continued; "When I was about eight, there was an occasion when I 'flew' down the street to my family home. I don't recall who or what was in control of my 'taking to the air', and when I went inside and told my mother, she laughed and said 'it was only my imagination.' I felt cheated by this comment, and was frustrated because I seemed to be the only one who could grasp this experience as reality. I felt alone."

Patty contacted her father 'James', still living on Waiheke, who rang me, quite anxious to talk to someone, away from the Island, whom he could trust and confide in. He also put me in contact with M.W. (since moved to Australia) who admitted to being the 'area manager' and confirmed much of what James said. It was invaluable to my research, over many years, to finally get first-hand verification of the 'project' from one of the senior scientists and facilitators.

James was able to tell me much more about the 'farm'. M.W. was rather lonely and found it hard to fraternise with the locals on the Island. He had become firm friends with James over a twenty-five-year period, and in fact they saw each other most days. James would have a communal, weekly breakfast with him and a couple of the 'group', until M.W.'s wife 'put a stop to it.'

"She, in fact, was the real one 'in charge', but M.W. told me a lot of what had really been going on up there over the years. Apparently after World War 2 a group of ex-German Nazis lived on the Island. One of them was a 'Swedish' scientist, a woman who experimented on 'rats', but we suspected it was humans. She often went to L.P.'s place and was part of his group. A friend of mine, said she had spoken to someone in German, expressing guilt over the Nazi experiments.

"The entire group was originally made up of U.S. military people and scientists, working with advanced electronics to make contact with aliens. I think there was even more to this, there was a definite agenda which I was not told about," James confided. "I don't know how successful they were, but certainly the Waiheke residents reported a lot of sightings in the 1970s. One UFO entered the water near a small island on Church Bay. I also saw lights over that area.

"Once I saw a scientist coming down from where the Experiment was being conducted, and I will never forget his face – it was ashen! The children who lived on this property, (now adults), still talk about this and Patty could tell you about what they said, as she is their age. At that time, I was living here, but not yet part of the experiments."

After a while a second project was begun using meditation or the power of the mind. This secondary project claimed that they succeeded in several UFO landings. In the late 1970s L.P. (connected to the U.S. military) who was more involved in the electronic experiments, moved to Australia, rather than back to the U.S. In the 1980s M.W. moved to the village, and it seems a secondary project continued for many years. M.W.'s Mexican wife was involved with the Gurdjeiff movement, which although only playing just one part of the experiments, incorporated a form of meditation which 'made all quiet inside' and 'blocked out the past and future'.

Both James and M.W. were very cagey about some details, but admitted they had contacted UFOs all the time on the island. The initial project was a secret U.S. Government (Electronic) Experiment to contact their 'friends'. It was much more complex than anyone realised, and sometimes done simultaneously with the U.S.

Both scientists commented that there is so much we don't understand as to how the universe works, and that often our perception of the physical world depends on our state of mind and spirit. Not only did they use Earth-energy Ley Lines, they also encompassed sounds, vibrations and levels of mental and spiritual perception.

The night the UFO had landed below Patty's grandmother's house they had been broadcasting a tape of 'alien vibrations.' They also divulged that data from famous New Zealand researcher, Bruce Cathie, who had specialised in Harmonics, had also been involved, but he was later silenced and ridiculed.

(This brought to mind the experiments documented by Dr Steven Greer – also essentially CE5s – where in 1973 he discussed a method of 'not only sounds and light, but also non-local consciousness and directed coherent thought, to communicate with extraterrestrial beings and their electronic devices'. He also described methods including not just telepathy, but also technology. A technological interface device, with specialised physics and electromagnetism, was also used, and later formed a basic part of psychotronic weapons systems.)

James and I corresponded by 'snail-mail', and spoke on the phone for some years before his death. He asked me not to contact him by electronic mail, as he didn't want any 'sensitive' information to be examined by the 'Government Surveillance Echelon Computer'. James imparted some confidential information to me, tutored me in some of the alien contact methods, and wanted me to go to the Island for further knowledge. Unfortunately, family circumstances prevented me from travelling to New Zealand.

James explained, "I should also detail how, as a westerner, I come to know these methods so well. My father was in China when the Japanese invaded and he rescued a Chinese Master and brought him to England. As a result of this, I have practised Shuichuan since early childhood and know all three styles of the subject very well."

James continued; "These beings are so far ahead of us and have a different state of consciousness. They communicate in a state of peace and mindlessness, and often can be reached through, dance, music and song, which can produce an amazing aura of intensity and energy."

(Australian aboriginal elders have explained to me that some of their sacred knowledge was, in part, that the 'vibrations' in their song, dance and instruments enabled contact with entities.)

While James admitted he had friends who had been abducted, and aliens were certainly present during some parts of the 'project', he was reticent about his own possible experiences. "Now, I can't say if I was abducted, but probably was. Since coming to New Zealand I seem to be compelled to live on Waiheke Island, which is an important place for Alien activity. I do curious intuitive things which have no explanation; perhaps I was 'programmed'. They appeared once at my house, and seemed to be examining it with some weird equipment. I was not afraid, and I don't recall them affecting me. I used my Qigong and was in a peaceful state. I think that is what they require to make contact with us, peace and mindlessness, for this is the way they are."

He admitted to using a form of Qigong and an Indonesian meditative exercise called 'Latihan', which had also been part of the second project. I began to realise, even though James denied it, he not only must have played a significant role in the second project, he in all probability helped initiate it. It was most probable that second project comprised not only elements of Gurdjieff practices – (which originated with the Russian Ivanovich; 1866-1949) – and James' input of ancient Eastern knowledge, but some components of the scientific electronic experiments.

(A lot of new questions and possible insights had arisen. There is so much about the Universe that we don't understand. Our perception of the physical world depends on both our state of mind and spirit. Why do some people see UFOs and not others? When they got them to land or appear, were they being attracted or manifested?)

James admitted to knowing of a future Earth cataclysm, and the reason for the visitation of the aliens. This had in part been confirmed by M.W., to both him and me, and it was more a natural disaster he was articulating, rather than warfare. One of the objectives of these particular aliens was to assist us through difficult times. "Alien abductions are the result of a beneficial need on their part to preserve colonies of human beings (of good spiritual quality), so that our race continues to survive and move forward." I have thought long and hard and decided it would be irresponsible to divulge any further details.

It is not known how much the events and experiences were affecting Patty's mother, but she was 'falling apart'. James and Becky were divorced, in fact she was frantic to get off the Island. With James's encouragement, Patty, Becky and her mother had all left New Zealand and moved to Australia. He was happier when they relocated to the Blue Mountains west of Sydney. He felt if the predictions were correct, they would be safer there.

Gillian had felt compelled to return to Waiheke Island in August 1999. She didn't know why, but felt she had some purpose there. Patty and Mark went back to visit James in November 1999, and they all met up in the pub, where Mark and Patty were singing in their band.

Gillian reminisced; "It was so strange, a lot of others were there, people we had gone to school with. It was like something had simultaneously drawn us all to come back at the same time. Many of our contemporaries were very musical, it was something in the notes and rhythm, and we all felt this tremendous bond and connection with each other.

(From the beginning of time, acoustic phenomena – sound, pitch, rhythm, frequency, vibration, resonance – have all been known to produce an amazing effect and outcomes in unimaginable ways.)

"I met Patty and Mark the next day, and we discussed the farm, or the 'Large House' as we called it, and what had happened in the past. We went up there, however new roads and subdivisions were on some parts of the property. As we drove around, we were stunned by the strong physical and emotional responses we felt in some areas. The old energy grids were still there."

Patty gave a sigh: "When we were in-line with my grandmother's old house weird things and strong physical effects started to happen. The radio turned on by itself, and I felt a tingling in my arms and hands. There was a tight pressure above my eyes and nose, like a force-field was blanketing my head. I started to get woozy and lightheaded."

Gillian continued; "We went around the road to a lower spot, further down – a hollow where we used to play as children. It was odd, L.P. used to let me play with his kids down there, but was paranoid about letting any adults into the area. Then I realised that the remains of what I had thought was a woolshed, was in fact more like a military barracks or bunker.

"I felt drawn to the area, but by this time both Mark and Patty were feeling very nervous, drained and exhausted."

Gillian confided that since the trip with Patty and Mark she had gone back to that spot to sit and meditate, usually feeling the same side-effects. She had several friends on Waiheke of Maori origin, who had recounted alien abductions. (Gillian never discussed her presence on the farm when the aliens visited, but she asked if I could arrange a hypnotic regression for her, later on.)

Gillian took one couple who were psychic and sensitive – familiar with indigenous knowledge and understanding. They went individually and separately to the spot to see if they could discern or recall any information. Dawn and Jean both felt nauseous in the area, as did Noel, their friend who was more scientifically minded. Jean was quite sick for several days afterwards. The consensus was that the anomaly was not an object, transportation device or portal area. Instead there was a 4-dimensional 'energy field' located under the area, which was to help humanity, and would activate during a particular transition phase, due to occur in the next few years.

Any further questions they had were blocked as the timing was not right. Gillian later decided it was important to return to and remain on the island. She felt compelled to stay on Waiheke as she had a 'purpose', but didn't know what it was. Later, she just disappeared; nobody knows where she is! Dawn thought Gillian was 'not completely human and had a specific task in relation to this'.

Noel said that during the intervening period some people, who had roles to play in relation to the site, would come to the Island. He also warned it was vital that none of this became public knowledge for some years, and I promised Gillian I would not release any information about Waiheke for at least ten years. Although Gillian has since 'disappeared', I have waited fifteen years, until

James died. (Much too young, though I don't know if this was connected with his activities.)

Whilst several islanders saw, or even had close contact with UFOs, few, if any reports reached the mainland.

On 8th August 1970, Tony O.Meara, an architectural draftsman, was on his way between Whitford and Maraetai Beach, four miles away, across the water, when he saw, in the clear blue sky, a metallic object over the island. It looked lenticular, disc-like in shape – both upper and lower surfaces convex – and 'was rocking from one side to the other', whilst glinting in the sun. He watched it hovering for about six minutes until he turned into his friend's driveway. By the time his friends left the house, and walked to a suitable vantage point, the strange craft was nowhere to be seen.

In 1978, Fred Dickeson received a letter from one resident, who had seen several unusual lights moving in the sky above. Several resembled a long, thin, dark object, similar to the 'lead out of a pencil'. She made note of the fact that more often than not they were visible on a Friday evening, when she took the dog out into the garden before retiring.

(It is probably an irrational thought on my part, but in those days the working week was Monday to Friday. Were some of the 'visitors' taking some 'rest and recreation' on the weekends?)

After moving to Australia, Patty had several more experiences, which I discuss in my book, *'The Alien Gene'*.

While this was only one of the 'generational' scenarios, as an investigator, I found it to be one of the most astounding cases I had ever researched. Many of the details were corroborated my multiple witnesses, including the people involved in the original scientific project

---

Part Two

The use of regressive hypnosis, to enable witnesses to recover the 'missing time' from their experience, has always been controversial. In Britain, some UFO organisations totally banned its use after the relatives of one witness successfully sued the UFO researchers for causing him psychological harm.

Other investigators, like myself, will only condone hypnotic regression to 'fill in' the blanks in otherwise conscious recall. (It is frequently argued, and often contentious,. as to whether what the witness 'remembers' is an accurate account of events and conversations, which can be inadvertently affected by the subject's previous knowledge or information regarding 'alien abductions'.)

The investigator must also ensure that the hypnotist is also both qualified and ethical. I know of two cases in the past, one in Britain and one in Australia, where the practitioner, unbeknown to either the researcher or the abductee, divulged information to unauthorised third parties.

In my last book, *"UFOs and Aliens – The Good Old Days'* I wrote of how, U.S. investigator, Jerome Eden, wrote to Fred Dickeson, advising extensive precautions be taken when a 'contactee' is under hypnosis to recover suppressed memories. He claimed he had evidence that the aliens could also interfere with hypnotic sessions when researchers were attempting to regress a witness.

Lee Robinson

This possibility, once thought unlikely, became of concern to North Island's *'NZSSRG'*. They wrote about this disturbing incident in their 1978 *'Spaceview'* newsletter.

'Readers of our last issue will remember the case of the Auckland North Shore woman who saw a UFO and lost half an hour. Well, we eventually submitted Lee to hypnotic regression, and as it turned out, she was apparently taken onto the small craft, and either transported physically or astrally to a larger craft.

'She went through much distress due to the lack of ability on the part of the hypnotist and his insatiable desire to pry information from the witness, which she insisted the hypnotist wasn't ready to know, morally. As it turned out, at the end of the session, we found he had already jacked up a journalist, ready to pass on the story to. Unfortunately, 'Sunday News', hashed up a story that was said to have come from 'Spaceview', about Lee's remembered experiences, and 'hashed up' was the catch phrase.

'This event caused Lee to decide that other than the few facts that I am including here, the rest will only be passed onto others as she feels impressed to do so.

'In her talks with the two aliens she met, she was told that 'they are bringing the Light to Earth for New Age Awareness', of which Lee had no prior knowledge. This seems to be a common factor in many contactee cases today......

'A point or two of interest to those in the U.S. who use a lot of hypnotic regression techniques; I observed the whole of Lee's re-enactment and was also aware of other forces that were present at the same time.....

'When the hypnotist asked about where the aliens came from, Lee said they never told her. Again she was asked, and again she aid she didn't know. Other questions were asked, and then the hypnotist asked again about the alien's planet of origin. "No", the subject began, and then said they came from the planet 'Zardia'.

'At that point, I became suspicious, and asked my spiritual guides what was going on. They said that false information had to be fed at this point to quench the desire of the hypnotist, who at times showed himself to be quite crazed at the idea of obtaining knowledge that others didn't have access to.

'Later in the piece, where Lee was telling the hypnotist that she would not give off further information, after considerable brow-beating by him, she was becoming so distressed, an entity impressed me that they would take over and bring the subject out of the trance. She then began saying repeatedly; "I am coming out of your control", until the hypnotist said; "Okay", and told her to wake up.

'NZSSRG' concluded by saying; *'Who is really in control of hypnosis sessions? The operator, the subject, or some unseen beings? This case alone, showed me that, unless the individuals concerned can handle what is to be given without any thought for self, then undoubtedly there have been many distortions of stories, unbeknown to witness and hypnotist alike.'*

When I worked in Australia with Fred and Phyllis Dickeson's son, Bryan, we usually employed the services of qualified, respected professionals when researching these cases. Many years later, after leaving New Zealand, Bryan wrote the following article;

'Using Hypnosis When Interviewing UFO Witnesses'

Background: My first attempt at hypnotically regressing a UFO witness, took place in April 1978. I was returning home from a UFO Convention in

Tauranga, New Zealand, and stopped off in Gisborne for a day or so. Five months beforehand, the Gisborne-Waimata area had experienced the most intense series of UFO events seen in New Zealand since the Kelso 'airship' sightings of 1909. I had worked with the local UFO groups for some months, but from afar, by telephone – from Wellington, some 400km south of Gisborne.

'That evening, I was presented with two of three witnesses, who, one night had experienced something bizarre, something terrifying, while keeping watch on a hillside in the Waimata Valley – the local UFO hotspot. One of the women, formidable, was prepared to be hypnotised.

'At the time I was familiar with the Betty and Barney Hill case in the U.S.A. and the Peter and Francis incident in South Africa. I had also seen someone perform hypnosis, but only as a party trick. In Gisborne I was surrounded by some twenty-five people, all looking at me intently – the itinerant drop-in 'UFO expert' – waiting to see what I would do next. – I was young – I was tired – I was stupid, and I was scared witless.

'Hypnosis was attempted that evening – twice. The event was revisited, but not entirely successfully. An account appeared in my parents Xenolog publication some months later. It emerged that two of the women had been taken on board a flying craft, subjected to medical examination, told 'stuff', then returned to their hillside. This 'abduction type' experience is now considered thoroughly normal within UFO studies. My first attempt at hypnosis was far from ideal, but I found the results intriguing.

'Since then, I have always felt bad about not performing that regression properly, and not providing enough support for the women involved. (If only I'd known what I know now). As a technique, hypnosis showed great promise, but the procedure requires expertise and some training – something that's often rare in UFO circles. In 1978, the problem of acquiring the necessary skills seemed insurmountable.

'For the next two decades I collected case data, especially on hypnosis techniques and their effectiveness. The topic was a difficult one – clinical hypnosis and hypnotherapy were then a very closed shop, (for a host of entirely valid reasons), and often seen as more closely related to devil worship than to either science or medicine. I found the amount of cautionary information available more than twice that of affirming material.

'However, hypnosis does help with day-to-day problems like weight loss and nicotine addiction, and has long addressed a boutique market. As such, it remains an expensive procedure.

'Meanwhile, I moved to Australia in late 1978, and during the 1990s was part of 'UFO Research (NSW)' in Sydney. In the early 1990s 'UFOR (NSW)' set up an Abductee Support group, but the savage politics and volatility, associated with abductee research, have always been a challenge.

'The Real Deal: An opportunity arose in the late 1990s for some formal training from a hypnotherapist who routinely worked with N.S.W. police. He had also trained police personnel to use hypnosis to help witnesses to recall some crime scene details, under strictly controlled and supervised conditions. This was a major opportunity for UFOR,NSW, to obtain proper expertise and reduce the trouble, expense and politics of finding qualified and sympathetic hypnotherapists prepared to work with UFO abductees.'

(Bryan went on to detail how he, and two other investigators, undertook a formal training course, and received certification upon successful conclusion.)

'...I still don't use hypnosis routinely – I'm hesitant/reluctant and don't promote it over other evidence-based investigation techniques. That's part of my science training – the idea of rummaging through someone's memories so closely, seems intrusive – just too 'up close and personal' to encourage the sort of objectivity which most serious ufologists aspire to. However, it can work spectacularly with witness recall, and hypnosis does help abductees better manage any trauma that may be present.

'......My differentiation into two types – 'UFO-sighting-only' and 'on-board-experience' events, is somewhat arbitrary. You will find a full spectrum of interactions. Any UFO report of something other than a 'distant light in the sky', involves extra complexity. Sightings I previously thought of as 'random' 'casual' or 'opportunistic events' are probably not so.

Bryan, who is one of the most ethical investigators I have ever known, went on to outline in detail all the precautionary measures a hypnotist must employ when interacting with a subject. Besides outlining the trauma suffered by genuine cases, and the first 'do them no harm' protocol, he also added the cautionary note;

'I am also surprised by those people who want to be abducted by aliens. In some UFO groups an increase in status may be anticipated, or they may be seeking attention, or just plain lonely. Hypnosis can become a way of validating or confirming an experience by conferring bragging rights. Fortunately, this is not common, but it does occur. It creates controversy, it wastes your valuable research time, and it can affect your research credibility.'

Bryan also went on the outline the errors of practitioners who ask leading questions or put pressure on the experiencers, to confirm the therapist's personal beliefs. He added; *'I would prefer that fully trained professionals – medicos and psychiatrists – could provide this procedure in a more accessible, affordable, appropriate way, However, I know experiencers who have tried the professional approach in the past, but have been temporarily fobbed of with psychotropic drugs, because the 'UFO stuff' was too weird, too unprofessional to manage.'*

CHAPTER TEN

Mr.X

In *'The Days of the Space Brothers'*, I wrote about New Zealand contactee Mr. X., who lived in Timaru. In the early 1960s he originally had a couple of rare physical contacts with the 'visitors', who called themselves his 'Two Friends' and usually left him written messages. They also urged him to practice and develop the art of telepathy.

This was a different approach from the open contacts practised by the 'Space Brothers' during the previous decade. Perhaps it was to avoid detection or capture by the authorities, who by that time were well aware of their presence. It must be noted that all the contacts, in the early days, were encouraged to learn and practice the art of telepathy. Even George Adamski had also urged his followers to develop this ability.

Mr. X's experiences started on 29th August 1960, when he saw an unusual object in the northern sky. It was a dark, cylindrical shape, emitting 'sparks'.

On 19th September, there was a knock on Mr. X's door at 10.30pm. Outside were two well dressed strangers – one was about thirty years old and the other fifty or so. The older one did the talking.

He said; "Good evening Mr........" and went on to say how pleased they were to have attracted his attention the other night. They had called to assure him that they would contact him later. They also said that they had tried to attract his attention several times before, but failed to do so.

As a joke, Mr. X said to them; "You wouldn't be Space People would you?"

There was no reply, but they smiled broadly at each other. Mr. X then asked them if they knew a certain Mr........, they answered they did, but that it was not necessary to see him because he did not need to be convinced. Mr. X then said; "You wouldn't be having me on, would you?" To this their expressions changed completely to ones of perplexity.

Mr. X then invited them inside. They refused, saying they had an important appointment to keep in a country district. They assured Mr. X that he would be hearing again from them shortly, said goodnight, and departed.

While they were with him he had no fear. They were ordinary well-spoken human beings – more like old friends. Later he became agitated, thinking he may have dreamt the whole meeting. He also wanted to know why they should pick on him, as he had always been a sceptic, and did not believe all he had read about UFOs. He said that he just would not accept it until he had further proof. Proof that he could touch or hold in his hands.

On 24th September, Mr. X found one note under his door, confirming their visit. It answered a number of questions which Mr. X had pondered over but had never spoken to a living soul. Mr. X was confused, and still not fully convinced. He showed the letter to the Dickesons, who photographed it, noting that the handwriting was different to that of Mr.X's. (Something they continued to do from then onwards, as they started including the information in their regular publications.)

The September communication read as follows; '*Mr...... – We write this on material which is hurriedly available to us. It is because of your stand in not accepting every thought blown about by the winds of wishful thinking, that we have decided to treat you as trustworthy. To men in your own circle of friends you have been thought to be luke-warm in your belief re certain things.*

'*You have not grabbed at every story concerning us. Indeed, it is because of this that we have approached you after a long period of observation. We now have every faith in your ability to use wisely these powers of discernment and discretion.*

'*We ask you not to become afraid because you suddenly find yourself in a position quite new to you. As promised, we shall see you again, and if further progress is made, your reward in this life will be made a real one in which very few have so far participated. In kindness to you, we have not told you who we are, because if we had, we would have broken your faith, since when things are a known certainty, there is no longer a need to have faith in them.*

'*We cannot openly reveal ourselves because of hostile surroundings, and we request that you do likewise, and that is why we say – "tell no man". Other things will be revealed to you according to your progress. Time is now fast running-out and our responsibilities become heavier as the focal point is reached.*

'P.S. We leave the use of this epistle safely to your own discretion, and which we personally delivered at your address by a friend of ours. Lastly, it is not what you thought, but is the power of levitation, which is as old as time itself. This is your answer to the question which has bothered you for some time, and that distance and time have no relation to us.

'No. we caused it to miss by over 1,000 miles. It was from a Godless nation, and that ground is Holy. It is now in a part of space, where we can deal with it at our leisure. Yes, that nation will be supreme for a short time.'

This was the answer to a question about something Mr. X had often pondered over, but had never actually spoken of to any living soul. The Dickesons immediately relayed the contents of the letter to George Adamski, who did not seem very enthusiastic about the turn of events.

Contactee, George Adamski, who more recently had been making outlandish statements, had fallen out of favour with the 'visitors'. He wrote to a colleague; *"There is a new group of space people that have replaced those who have been here for quite some time.... When new groups come in to help us, they present differently than the groups before them....I have not been informed what their ideas are, but I will sooner or later."*

Perhaps the 'Two Friends' were referring to George Adamski, when in one 1962 message to Mr. X they said; *'We are watching events with considerable interest as earthlings put projectiles into space, and we keep a check on all, allowing some and stopping the effect of others.*

'Many who started out well, and worked according to our plan have fallen by the wayside. They have worked by their own plans, and do no longer convey the truth to your world, but make fiction instead. It is for this reason that we turn to you, hoping that you will continue to proceed according to our plan, which we are sure you will. You are extremely fortunate that your friend is in a position to make known our messages as you receive them. We are fortunate that he is on the side of Truth. Truth, in the past, has been tampered with to make it sound more mysterious. We again stress the point that we are not exhibitionists – we do not do, nor say, many of the things which are said of us. Do not expect from us the impossible, because many statements of us are quite impossible even for us to carry out. As we have said, we are just human like you.'

In October 1961, the Space Brothers who wanted to negate some of Adamski's claims, wrote in a communication with Mr.X; *'...We are not from your System, but from a constellation or system near what earthlings call Sagittarius, which is very far from your position in space.....There is too much sensationalism written about us of which we are not capable. We again stress that we do not take earthlings for rides into the Creator's Heavens, and as you already know, if we have business to arrange, it is always done by appointment on your solid Earth, and we wish all earthlings to know this truth.*

'No humans exist on any of your neighbouring planets, and we say again that your planet is the most favoured. - Your Two Friends.'

They also conveyed to him other information which was contrary to that given by Adamski over the previous years, especially when they said there was no air nor water on the Moon, and that there was little difference from the side facing the Earth. In later years, after our first landing on the Moon in 1969, these statements proved to be correct, and Adamski's assertions erroneous.

(Although I believe George Adamski was genuine in the early days, many consider that once famous, he embroidered and fabricated his experiences with fanciful stories to enhance his significance.)

They also wrote; *'...Our people have been visiting your world for millions of years, even the Word of God tells you that. We say 'millions' because we were visiting it long before Humans were established here. If we were to give you the answers to all your questions....you would never have time for your own affairs, so we ask for your patience, as always. As promised, we know how much is good for you.'*

They also went on to correctly describe the environment on all the planets of the solar system, and how they were totally uninhabitable.

Contained in the October/November issue of the Dickesons' *'SSRG'* newsletter was a letter Mr. X had written; *'I have certain friends here in New Zealand, where I live, who have requested me to write about my attitude re space ships prior to recent happenings at my home.*

'I have never fully believed in such things, but now I am not so sure. These friends know what happened, because I told them everything. There is no need to relate it here. Sooner or later it will all be revealed, so until then I will merely be known as Mr. X for my own protection.

'I shall go no further, other than to say that I am now fully convinced that I was visited by two people from outside this world of ours. The facts of the occurrence have been proved because of a letter I received from my two visitors.....This letter is not the only occurrence. Other things happened which put it beyond all fiction.

'Ridicule is what I am afraid of! This is the last thing I want, so you can understand why I will not publicise my name. It matters little to me whether I am believed or not, as I do not want publicity. But I shall continue to work quietly if that be my destiny.

'I now have perfect faith in the two friends who paid me that visit. While in their company, I felt at perfect peace and had a feeling of wonderful satisfaction. I have never had a feeling like that before on meeting with strangers. This, and other things which happened, puts it beyond all doubt that I have had a privilege which makes me feel proud. I am not a man who can be bothered by fiction, and so do not even read such stuff, so I can assure you that you can believe all I have said.

'I now admit that I feel most humble, and yet a little guilty because I previously did not believe in such things.

I remain – Yours in truth – Mr.X.

When he got up, on the morning of 8th October, Mr. X found a note he had written earlier on a notepad on the table. It was in his own handwriting, and not that of the letter under his door.

'Date; 8th October 1960 – Time; 4am woke – couldn't sleep – made a cup of tea then took a walk to the front gate – 4.45am The eastern sky was showing a little lightness – breaking day. On the one side of the street two men – same as before were waiting. We had no sooner seen one another when they greeted me with;

"Good morning Mr.........., we are sorry to have disturbed your early morning slumber, causing you to come out at such an early hour."

'They then came across to my side of the street, shook hands and said that it is most important for me to try harder to project my thoughts outward as it could save them personal contact with me, which takes up much time and is dangerous to them.

'They said that I was receiving them faintly, but that they were still unable to receive me at all. If I would cultivate the art of thought transference, they would be able to give me directions on important matters....

'That's all that happened. They again shook hands and departed, walking fairly briskly away.'

On 14th November 1960, there was another note, which said in part... *'We know you will receive this note safely from your own box. We have a reason for working in this way, so thought we would advise you.....There is much ahead to be done and you will have much to overcome for many will not believe even as in the days of old. We shall advise you of any of our changes in our plans of contact, and if we have anything of an urgent nature, we shall see you personally.'*

On 8th December, there was another note, which amongst other things, congratulated him on his Birthday, something Mr. X and his family had forgotten about. *'We have not forgotten you. God bless you and all connected to you – not only today but every day. Your two friends.'*

A couple of weeks later, on 20th December, Mr. and Mrs. X were down at Caroline Bay, in Timaru, at about 3.30pm one afternoon. A very distinctive man approached and began talking to them. He looked to be about fifty years old, 5'8" tall and proportionately built. He had brown, brushed back hair, a high forehead and small moustache. He really stood out from the rest of the crowd, and was wearing sunglasses and a beautifully tailored green blazer.

His voice was low, quiet and cultured, and he started by commenting on how warm the water was, much better than Wainui Beach near Gisborne. When Mr. X asked the stranger if he came from Gisborne, he said no, he was only there for a short time.

Mr. X was going to do some reading while he sat on the shore, and was holding the book *'The Sky People'* by Brinsley le Poer Trench. The stranger asked if they were interested in the 'Sky People', and Mr. X handed him the book.

As he was talking to them the man kept running his fingers across the words on the bottom of the front cover – *'Visitors to this planet in Atlantean and Biblical times are with us today'*. He handed the book back and said; "I know all about it!"

During the conversation he said; "WE are very concerned about the world situation, they speak of the atomic threat in the abstract, as though it is a thing which is bound to happen."

Mr. X commented that it was just a matter of mankind pressing the button and bringing on his own destruction. Really, psychologically speaking, the world was mentally sick.

"You are quite right," the stranger agreed. He murmured something else in a foreign language, which almost sounded like symbols. He then spoke up in English, as if translating it. The original sentence was not any recognisable language to Mr. X, so he muttered a short reply in Esperanto. They all laughed, and the stranger departed.

During their conversation the couple asked him if he would be staying in Timaru, and he said not. When queried about belonging to any particular organisation, the stranger said he had no headquarters but 'travelled extensively'.

Mr. and Mrs. X were almost sure he was a 'spaceman'. Mr. X said, that although a different 'person', he had the same look about him as the 'friends' he had met before. Further conversation between them clearly indicated that he was no ordinary visitor to the Bay.

In 1970, Brinsley le Poer Trench published a report from Carol Halford-Watkins of 'Contact Canada'. This message, regarding telepathic communications, was of great interest to the Dickesons in New Zealand, as it tallied with one given to Mr. X.

Carol Halford-Watkins wrote; *'At the appointed time period we tuned in telepathically to the Space People with welcoming thoughts. My personal experience when, after this, I made my mind receptive to telepathic communication was that I received the following message:*

'The time is not yet right, nor is your world yet ready to receive us in any numbers for friendly personal contact. Isolated landings for contact with specifically selected Earth people, and the inevitable, odd accidental confrontations will continue to take place, but under cosmic law, we cannot present ourselves en-masse until there is a better spiritual climate on your planet, and a far greater sincerely expressed desire to meet with us on the part of Earth people.

'Do not be discouraged or give up these attempts to make contact with us. Rather, concentrate on building them up to the massive proportions required for a successful meeting with us. Your welcoming thoughts are being well received, and we are pleased with your efforts which are the first and necessary steps towards your desired meeting with us.

'Some of you are disappointed at the present apparent lack of our presence in your skies. Be not deceived; we have not deserted you, but are near you in great numbers although invisible to your earthly eyes. We have first a specific mission to perform, vital for your survival, but later we shall make ourselves known to you visibly in a spectacular manner. In the meantime, 'Contact' has our special blessing, and we ask you to link up with us in earnest prayers for planet Earth and its people.'

On 4th July 1961, M. X received another note, again encouraging him to learn and practise the art of telepathy, or 'mind transference', something that George Adamski had also advocated. They noted that; 'It is impossible to be with you personally each time we give you a message, so we must do it this way. Your world is in a very dangerous state, but we are watching it very closely. We may soon be replaced by two other brothers, but you would be contacted by them in place of us. This, we ourselves are not sure about. There is much sadness among us because of the plight of our worldly brothers.'

Mastering telepathy took Mr. X some time, but eventually he channelled, and wrote down, telepathic messages, some of which I reproduced in my book 'The Days of the Space Brothers'.

A few weeks later, on both 23rd July and just after midnight on 20th August, Mr. X received messages. It is worth noting that, at about the same time, George Adamski claimed receiving a similar message.

'Since atoms are the material out of which the Creator builds all things, and that man should use this same thing to destroy his handiwork, thereby throwing back into the Creator's face this same material, then Nations found guilty of so doing shall surely perish by the same means.

Hold this message until we instruct you further. God bless you.'

Immediately after receipt of this message Russia resumed nuclear atmospheric testing. On the night of 5th September, Mrs. X found the following note in their letterbox.

'We know that the test has failed. And that no more can be done along those lines. For nations now know the consequence which they themselves have admitted. We can do no more! But we shall advise you of our plans from time to time.

'You must expect disbelief and opposition from those who have no faith. Wisdom may yet prevail among the nations. There is much sadness among us because the innocent will suffer along with the guilty, yet help shall come in an unexpected form if necessary – so fear not.

'Seven ships were met during the test, and departed on their various ways immediately after the test was over. It was the first meeting of its kind ever to take place. We cannot do the impossible and sweep away the Will of the Creator, being human, just like you are, but we can help those who are willing.

'You may publish or make known this message if you care, it matters little now.'

'We are your two friends'

Whilst Mr. X rarely saw his visitors' space ships, he wondered if it was them on the afternoon of the 26th August 1962 when at 2.15pm, he and a close neighbour were out on his lawn, and saw something shining in the sky. It was a perfectly round object, with a dark round circle underneath. As they stared up, a second craft, at about the same altitude, was sighted. Higher up, two more were circling each other in a clockwise direction. All four glinted like mirrors in the sunlight. Within a short time they all vanished.

On 6th October 1962, Mr.X found the following note in his letterbox. Perhaps the 'visitors' were trying to impart a better understanding of their own nature and activities.

'We do not criticise the human race, since all are not without sin. We too are sinners – we too can die – we too have our accidents and get killed in crash accidents. We do not criticise earthlings. Who are we to criticise? There is too much sensationalism written about us, of which we are not capable. We again stress that we do not take earthlings for rides in the Creator's heavens, and as you already know, if we have business to arrange, it is always done by appointment on your solid earth, and we wish all earthlings to know this truth.

'No humans exist on any of your neighbouring planets, and we again say that your planet is the most favoured.'

A short time later, Mr.X found a second note in his mail box. *'It was only after today's first note was sent off to you, that this further thought came to us. It is, that we too have gone through experiences almost akin to earthlings, but we have risen above all that. We have advanced to the stage where we were able to break free from it. Man must learn the hard way from his own experience – there is no other way! He must experience something before he can understand it....Telling him doesn't help! He must experience it. That is the only way to learn.*

'Regret that you have been so worried at not hearing from us so often. There is no point in bothering either you or ourselves when there is nothing to deal with wherein you could be of assistance.

'God Bless you all – Your two friends.'

On 17th February 1963, Mr. and Mrs. X received another note; *'Rebellion has been threatening among certain cosmic entities which are even now moving in the direction of your location. We are doing our best to divert their direction of travel because if they come too close to your place in space, their influence will be tragic for your present uneasy peace, as past wars will be nothing to what this will cause if they succeed. We have been too busy with this cosmic trouble to communicate with you, but give this as a kindly warning that trouble may come your way. We hope to be strong enough to stop it. May the good Lord help us.*

'God bless you all and all who look for truth – Your two friends.'

(I wonder - were they referring to the 'bug-eyed greys', so prevalent in later years?)

In 1963, not many people knew that Mr. X and his wife had moved out into the country. At 10.15pm on 18th May, he noticed a note under the back door of his new home. It read; *'We knew that you had moved from your old address, and that disrupted our usual arrangements, so no messages have been left there.*

'We are having much trouble – grave troubles of which we spoke in our last note, delivered at that time by hand. You did see her – one of our opp-sex, and you may yet meet her. She was indeed fortunate in not being openly seen; this is for our own protection that we are able to do this.

'The note was delivered at that moment to give proof to all, that it is beyond your powers to be the author of these notes. We knew what was to be said, and by whom and knew it is truth. Yet we have that battle to deal with at present. Do doubters need more than that demonstration of timing-delivery. This is also for your protection and to strengthen you in the eyes of others. - Your two friends.'

On the night of 19th October, Mr X found the following note under his front door;

'We are not wishing to influence you if you do not desire, but believe us, we are working for the best interests of humanity. If you look into the heavens tomorrow night at 11.30pm, you will see our 'V' sign again to satisfy that we have not forgotten you. Soon, we shall prove beyond all reasonable doubt that we are true and steadfast in all our promises to you.

'If conditions are good, watch for us in your heavens at 11.30pm Monday from now. We honour your scatterer of news, Mr. Dickeson. There will be a terrible period shortly, but we shall be with you.' - 'Your two friends.'

The night of the 20th the sky was blocked by a dense fog, but at 11.30pm on Monday 21st October, Ron Davidson in Timaru went into his garden and saw an object coming fast from the south. It was a deep blue colour, and elliptical in shape. When almost overhead, it stopped and was joined by another craft which approached from the north. They hovered together, both giving off a bright flashing light, before moving slowly apart. One then departed to the east, and the other to the west, before returning and hovering over the centre of the city.

At 11.35pm, several witnesses in and around Timaru also reported similar sightings.

On 21st November 1963, another note was found under the door of their new home. (Shortly before, many witnesses had reported seeing multiple craft in the sky.) It said in part; *'...We expected to be called from duty with you long ago, but we are still with you and seems that may be for a long time yet. We are not the force of evil as some may brand us, but we know the ways of men and must expect opposition, nor do we have wings on our backs, nor fly like fowls in the air.*

'You have noticed how everything has dropped into place for you since you have known us – and so it will be for your world if it will look our way. Our

display was not intended for you in particular, but to convince doubters. You need no convincing – you have met us – know us – spoken with us! We have already dispelled your doubts. Do not weaken! Be strong. Be steadfast. Be not be led astray by would-be or seemingly scientific writings!

'God bless you and all who are with us – Your two friends.'

On 25th June 1964, Mr. X received another letter; *'We have been long in writing to you, but we have been fighting a terrible battle, only partly successful. Many evil ones have broken through and are now at work on your Earth. We cannot foretell the result as we ourselves do not know yet. But you may expect trouble at any time. If so, we shall be seen in your skies in greater numbers as we shall be there to help. If the following sign is seen it will be the warning of trouble. Watch your skies for this 'Z' and know that we are not far away. These evil ones have already influenced one we trusted. They will spoil those in higher places. - Your Two Friends'*

Fred and Phyllis Dickeson wrote the following report about the next incident:

'On the evening of January 13th, 1965, we called on Mr. and Mrs. X at their home, and after a very enjoyable evening watching TV, the conversation eventually turned to the two Space Friends and the fact that it had been a very long time since we had heard anything from them.

(Unbeknown to anyone at the time, seven 'flying saucers' were seen by a Qantas aircrew, and tracked by their and ground radar, flying in a 'V' formation towards New Zealand at an altitude of 45,000ft. The media reported that top-secret investigations, to determine their identity, were being conducted by the RAAF and the RNZAF.)

'After we had left for home Mr. X took his milk bottles out to the gate, and while there, for some unknown reason, he checked his letter box. To his surprise, he found a note inside from the Two Friends. He went back into the house, and once he and his wife read the note, he immediately began calling our telephone number.

'When we reached home, some fifteen minutes later, we could hear the phone ringing, and as is always the case, it stopped when we were about to pick it up. However, a few minutes later Mr. X called again. The note he had received read as follows:

'Take up your pen and write, for we shall guide you each time you do this. We shall not allow you to make a mistake in the knowledge given to you. We can give you more this way. When you feel the urge to write – write! We shall guide you in each word! There is much to tell that this world should know. We will have a strong knowledge of what is not truth, and we shall know all that you write. This is all part of our promise to you. You may think it to be your own work, but it will not be so, so as with your music, which was never your own work.'

'Your two friends.'

'You can imagine how dumbfounded Mr. X was after he read the note out to us.

'He said, "What do they expect me to do? It's a pretty tall order!"

'As usual, after a discussion we came to the conclusion that none of us could do anything. We just had to wait and see what happened next.

'It was not long, however, before Mr. X was sitting down at his typewriter. Amazingly enough he just began typing with no thought of whatever or what was coming next. He said that he just doesn't have to think – he just writes! He can get up and leave it for a spell, then come back, read the last sentence, and then he is off again.

'Just what people will think about the information contained in these writings is hard to imagine. We think a great many will not, or could not, possibly believe what has been written, and yet there will be some who will know, deep down, somewhere in the subconscious that it is true.

'We must admit that we too had great difficulty in digesting and absorbing the information given. However, we have our part to do, and so we print the writings and leave it to the reader to either accept or reject, depending on whatever degree of understanding they have reached.

'If these are really truth, then we have no hesitation in eventually believing that they will prove correct as time goes on....With no further comment, we leave you, the reader. To evaluate the information contained herein as you see fit. We feel it just cannot be read through, it must be studied and reasoned out.'

On 27th, 28th and 29th July 1971, several witnesses had reported a large golden glow shining very brightly in the sky. It moved slowly and silently, later appearing to land in the distant foothills. On 29th July, Mr. X received another visit from two Space Friends.

At 7.30pm there was a knock on the door, and Mr. and Mrs. X immediately asked them in. Mr. X recognised his visitors as the same two men that he had met all those years ago. He shook their hands and said; "I know you!'

One replied; "You ought to – we met you early one morning, years ago."

This was the first time Mrs. X had seen them, and was impressed with the two well dressed men in neat suits, (no hats), with eye-catching shoes – an indistinguishable red-grey colour with a metal clasp up the centre. The older man was taller, and did most of the talking. The younger man was shorter, and had a somewhat round face. Their visitors politely declined to come in, and said they would be in contact within a few days.

The Dickesons had noted it was only on rare occasions, since 1960, that they had appeared in person. During the ensuing years they had usually kept contact with him and the Dickesons through notes being left either under the door or in his letterbox. One of the notes had mentioned that if they had anything of an urgent nature, they would contact him personally.

Communicating in this manner may have seemed strange to some, but had proven more accurate in conveying the message. Word of mouth could result in important points being forgotten, confused, coloured by retelling or interpretation and generally unwittingly distorted. Further, Mr. X and the Dickesons had photographed each note after it was received.

A few days later, on 3rd August, 1971, Mr. X found the following handwritten note in his letterbox.

'This is bad news, but we will be compelled to abandon all our attempts to help earthlings to a better way of life. Even our own brothers are not safe amongst you. One of our most trusted and loved Brothers has been murdered by earthlings while doing his duties. We have been recalled to our own sphere, and given instructions to break-off all contacts in the meantime.

'All the good we have done has been set-back to nothing in almost every case. No sooner than we put something right, then it is immediately put to nought by vested interests. We can almost smell the stench of your society, your political jostling for high places, your corrupt monetary system, your badness morally.

'Political untruths flow with the greatness of ease from the tongues of rulers throughout your world, and even your League of Nations is powerless to prevent iniquity in your world. It is powerless because it is composed of these very same elements of which we speak.

'We saw and spoke with you a few nights ago, yet there may still be the chance that we shall have need of your kind help, but how long it will be we cannot even guess at the moment. And now you understand why we made this last personal visit to you, and this last time so that your wife could be present.'

'We shall watch over you'
'Your two friends'

In September 1971, the Dickesons wrote to a friend with contacts in Holland and Brazil who had advised that although some 'visitors' still remained here, the UFOs were withdrawing most of their people off Earth. They also noted that there were several sightings, from Oamaru on the South Island, of four craft on the days just before the 'Xs' were visited. Other reports had come from Palmerston North, Kapiti Island and Dunedin. Whatever was 'going on', something was happening in our skies!

In August 1973, Mr. X was distressed when he received the following note; *'We are sorry, but we must find someone else who is prepared to write – Your Two Friends.'*

He rang the Dickesons, who had also received a similar note under their own door, with a postscript asking them not to tell Mr. X – they would do that themselves. Whilst the Dickesons realised that Mr. and Mrs. X were very frail both mentally and physically, they commented that – 'it was such a cold dismissal – very strange!'

In 1975 the Dickesons reflected upon the entire Mr. X saga. The situation was not unique - there had been other 'X Cases' around the world, and two more of the 'overseas leaders' had confirmed that 'space people' were being taken off the earth.

They well understood that some researchers will reject a particular event because it does not fit with their personal belief in how the UFO phenomena should be. They believed that any theory or belief should be examined to the extent both its strengths and weaknesses became apparent.

Some colleagues had become quite hostile, saying George Adamski was genuine and Mr. X was not. There were even differences of opinion in the Dickesons' own group and family, however, the 'two friends' had expressed their appreciation and approval of the Dickesons publishing the information in their newsletters, where they said; *'We, on the other-hand, felt as unbiased investigators, we had to look at all angles, and disclose the truth as we found it, regardless of anything else. We are seeking the truth – that has always been our policy.*

'There are at least four 'X notes' not published at all. Two referred to personal matters involving the Xs or ourselves, and were of little use to those not directly concerned.... Some we could not cope with in a public context at all....

'Besides the Two Friends' notes, there were also the 'X Writings'- three very long and involved, apparently inspired pieces. We published very limited copies of these under separate cover. The few which we did produce deeply disturbed some of our older members, and our credibility in some quarters. There was nothing about the 'guiding angels from God leading us out of sin, or the usual spiritual fringes to the messages received from George Adamski and others.'

Earlier, in 1969, realising that many were sceptical, Fred Stone, who had himself spent time with Mr. X, published the following statement in his Australian *'Paranormal'* newsletter; *'Mr. X is a fine man, living in the South Island of New Zealand, and near the Dickesons. Your editor met him when he was touring there, giving lectures, and can state he is a fine gentleman who very much impressed your editor as being completely honest and certainly would never attempt deceit himself.*

'For quite a few years he has had strange letters left in his box, which are signed always 'your two friends'. These letters, quite a few your editor has personally seen, are certainly not the handwriting of Mr. X, or faked by him. Apart from this, I am positive that Mr. X did receive them as stated.

'I have never questioned the honesty or integrity of Mr. X. If any deceit is possible, it is certainly not him, however there are those who have suspected the 'two space friends' to be a hoax, or deceiving Mr. X. This is something which must be decided by the reader for himself. Your editor suggests that the reader accepts him at face value, and from those who have personally met him as being a very humble man indeed, who merely relays what he has received.'

Fred Stone, however, found any telepathic communications, no matter how genuine in their transmission to Mr. X, to be dubious in regards to their origin. Across the world, British researcher, Tony Dodd, received similar telepathic messages to those of Mr. X.

He reported one of those messages to *'OVNI'*; *'Our presence in your Solar System is to observe the evolution progress and environmental changes occurring not only in your planet, but to its people.*

'Using this observational technique enables us to foresee potential future difficulties which may arise, and if necessary, give you a view on the course of action needed to overcome them. To achieve these aims, we employ the use of many types of monitoring equipment, each with a responsibility for a different area of investigation.

'The problems facing your race are many and are largely due to the act of your technology being turned towards the hostile acts of humanity. You have the ability to turn the world into a place of harmony and plenty, if you direct your abilities and enterprise towards sharing, with not only your own people but the natural laws of the universe. You can advance technology, but only for the good of all, otherwise it will destroy you.

'We are here with the hand of brotherly leadership, to teach you as you evolve. Each one of your kind has the ability to grow in cosmic consciousness. The answer lies in the fabric of you all. We have great love for you, and know that the direction is now turning toward the path of cosmic understanding.

'But we can only advise. The future of your race must be determined by your own free will. Our view of you shows great hope and expectation, and we await with anticipation, the day when you aspire to the Federation of Cosmic Brotherhood.'

I, and other researchers, have often wondered if the frequencies in some musical compositions can transmit 'messages, or 'information'. In 1964, the previously mentioned Australian researcher Fred Stone, also a contactee, was visiting Timaru, and spent an evening with Mr. X and New Zealand researchers - the Dickesons. He later commented; *'Mr. X is a great musician and composer. He claimed the 'Space People' had inspired many of his compositions. Half way during the evening he said he felt moved to improve a piece of music – a simple composition which had just come floating through his mind. He went to the piano and began playing. Suddenly I felt myself also being moved, and as each note was played, I knew what was coming and began to hum the tune as though I had known it all the while. At the end I asked Mr. X if he knew the name of the tune, and he replied that - no he didn't know – what was it?*

'Without thinking I said "Dedication'- there are verses to it. Play it again." He returned to the piano, and as he replayed the theme, the verses came into the mind telepathically from the Space Brothers, who were unseen, yet present. This was witnessed by everyone present at the time.

'Surely this was evidence that we two men were being moved together in unison to be instruments of service. Maybe you may not be impressed by this account, or feel it was a proof of the genuineness of either party, but one had to be present to know what was felt and transpired in that room. We were not being moved by our own powers, but from those of a much higher source.'

Mr. X's 'music' has intrigued me. Perhaps he was unwittingly channelling it and passing on more information and inspirational contact from his 'two friends'. Our bodies and cells react to sound – their vibrations and frequencies. Perhaps there were more messages being secretly transmitted within the pulse and harmonics of the notes.

In the U.S., George Van Tassel and his family also sang popular songs, and sometimes hymns to their guests under the Giant Rock. A couple who were visiting commented; "On one occasion they sang a certain song which Van had obtained directly from one of his space contacts. To us the music was very unusual, and the words were both simple and beautiful."

As an investigator, I have always found the claims of self-professed 'contactee', Howard Menger, to be very dubious. It is, however, interesting that he also claimed that although he could not play the piano, he was able to play music that the Space Brothers had taught him.

They explained that every note had a specific density and frequency which causes a sympathetic vibration when created at the correct frequency and in certain combinations. People hearing the themes would react in their conscious state with increased understanding and brotherly love toward one another.

Throughout history we have been aware of the hidden elements in sound and music. Acoustic phenomena – sound, pitch, rhythm, frequency, vibration, resonance – have all been known to produce an amazing effect and outcomes in unimaginable ways. In fact, these subliminal forces are far more powerful than most people realise.

By 1982, Mrs. X had passed away some time earlier, and Mr. X, now quite frail and in his eighties, had been admitted to a nursing home, as he did not want to be a burden to his two married children, who lived quite close.

In 1971, Fred and Phyllis Dickeson, who had received a lot of disapproval for supporting Mr. X, published the following testimony in their 'SATCU' newsletter.

'We, the editors, hereby testify that we have, at all times, in all sincerity and honesty, related the facts and happenings truthfully as they have occurred, we have not added to, or distorted any of the messages in the X case. Furthermore, Mr. X has been proved genuine and sincere in many and numerous ways, he has absolutely nothing to gain by making any fabrication in the story; neither would he be capable or bothered in perpetrating a hoax.'

They went on to say how they had received an enormous amount of criticism, which did not disturb them anymore as they had prayed for guidance that what they were doing was right.

'....Regardless, whether anyone can accept the story as Truth matters little, their thinking cannot alter what is true. We are in bondage to no man, we do not have to explain to anyone, or account to anyone, other than the Creator of all. Everyone has a universal link to each other, and must help their fellow man wherever possible.'

INDEX

G

H

I

J

K

L

M

www.ingramcontent.com/pod-product-compliance
Lightning Source LLC
Chambersburg PA
CBHW072128020426
42334CB00018B/1716